REFRIGERATOR CAR
Color Guide

Empty ice-bunker reefers ride west behind Union Pacific Big Boy #4007 on August 31, 1958.
(Lou Schmitz)

by
Gene Green

Copyright © 2005
Morning Sun Books, Inc.

All rights reserved. This book may not be reproduced in part or in whole without written permission from the publisher, except in the case of brief quotations or reproductions of the cover for the purposes of review.

Library of Congress
Catalog Card No. 2005924898
First Printing
ISBN 1-58248-165-2

Published by
Morning Sun Books, Inc.
9 Pheasant Lane
Scotch Plains, NJ 07076
Printed in Korea

Robert J. Yanosey, President
To access our full library *In Color* visit us at
www.morningsunbooks.com

DEDICATION

This book is dedicated to my wife Heide. My health over the last few years made it hard for me to work on this book. She helped me through that period and helped me get some work done and ultimately to finish it. I just couldn't have completed this task without her and I can't thank her enough for all she has done for me.

ACKNOWLEDGEMENTS

Refrigerator cars have always been among the more colorful railroad cars. Light colored paint was used to reflect heat. The usual colors were yellow or orange although there were other colors as we shall see within these pages. We had to decide what to include and what to exclude from the large volume of material submitted for this book. That is never an easy task so some rigid guidelines helped narrow the selection some. **First**, to be considered for this book, the refrigerator car had to be listed in the back of the *Official Railway Equipment Register* in the pages for PRIVATE OWNER CARS. Cars owned by railroads, and this includes Santa Fe's SFRD refrigerator cars, would not be included but cars leased by railroads from private owners could be included. **Second** the cars had to be equipped with ice bunkers or brine tanks. Beyond that the task was to choose the best pictures for the book. Even then it was not as easy as it may seem. The greater the number of slides we tried to include the smaller each picture would be reproduced. Large pictures means fewer pictures. There was compromise at every step. You, the reader, will judge whether we were successful or not.

Gratitude must be expressed to all the photographers who were trackside in years gone by to record what we see in this volume. Appreciation must also be expressed towards those who have collected the work of others and so willingly share their collections. Thanks to Bill Welch for help with the Fruit Growers Express, Burlington Refrigerator Express and Western Fruit Express sections. Jeff Koeller provided lots of good information and helped get the North Western Refrigerator Line section arranged in a logical order. Ed Hawkins provided detailed information on the refrigerator car design characterized by the horizontal seam on the sides. Jerry Hesley and Soph Marty came through at the last minute with additional slides that were needed to round out the coverage of icing facilities large and small. Lloyd Keyser can always be counted on to help with appropriate material and this book was no exception. My friend Jim Mischke contributed both slides and encouragement. Pete Heindel took on the role of research assistant and provided a huge stack of copies of magazine articles on various cars and companies in this book. Wayne Shubert told a number of interesting stories about exchanging heaters in refrigerator cars, and the dangers of such work, in the Twin Cities area. Bob Yanosey can always be counted on for direction when needed. Bob envisioned the theme of this book after viewing the unique series of car icing slides taken in Columbus by Paul Winters. This inspiration prompted him to ask me to write this book. For that I am very grateful!

TABLE OF CONTENTS

Introduction	3-5
Icing Refrigerator Cars	6-9
Icing Facilities	10-13
American Refrigerator Transit	14-21
Armour Co.	22-26
Cudahy Car Lines	27-29
Fruit Growers Express (Burlington Refrigerator Express Co. & Western Fruit Express Co.)	30-47
General American Transportation Corp.	48-50
Merchants Despatch Transportation Corp.	51-65
Morrell • Rath & Mather Stock Car Co.	66-73
North American Car Corp.	74-77
North Western Refrigerator Line Co.	78-83
Pacific Fruit Express	84-93
Railway Express Agency	94-95
Swift	96-103
Union Refrigerator Transit	104-120
Western Refrigerator Line	121-122
Wilson Car Lines	123-127
Epilogue	128

REFRIGERATOR CAR
Color Guide

The use of refrigerator cars probably reached its zenith as the depression ended in the late 1930s and during the 1940s. Thereafter trucks began to take away the traffic. Refrigerator traffic isn't gone completely though. As I write this in 2004 just in my town there is a local grocery warehouse that always has one or two mechanical refrigerator cars being unloaded.

The following is quoted from an article by an official of General American Transportation Corporation which appeared in the October 1937 issue of *Railway Mechanical Engineer*. This excerpt gives an impression of reefer traffic in its heyday.

"The following few items indicate the widespread production of perishables, and will doubtless impress you with the fundamental basis of special car operation to meet demands from widely separated sections of the country at various seasons of the year. Again the greatest influence is service to the producer, and this service has to be met in the most economical manner possible.

The most surprising bit of information is the fact that the railroads handle more tonnage of milk and milk products every year than they do of steel. A large volume of this milk was returned from trucks to the railroads when our company developed the glass lined bulk milk car.

Without including homemade or local production, several hundred creameries produce for rail transportation over a billion five hundred million pounds of butter, one-third of this coming from Minnesota, Iowa, and Wisconsin.

No one can even guess the total production of eggs, but the cities of New York, Chicago, Boston and Philadelphia annually receive by rail more than 6,500,000 cases of 30 dozen eggs per case. The largest egg producing state is Washington, followed by California, New York, Iowa and Illinois. Certainly this is a diversified business over a large territory.

Minnesota leads all states in dressed poultry production, and the four cities mentioned above receive between nine hundred million and one billion pounds annually by rail.

Potatoes lead the vegetable and fruit tonnage. Apples are second. Washington originates 40 per cent of all the apples shipped by rail. California ships 70 per cent of the oranges and 99 per cent of the lemons. The southern states-Florida to Arizona-are all increasing their productions rapidly.

Eighty-five per cent of the perishable products handled on rails are grown or produced west and southwest of Chicago and south of the Ohio river. The bulk of this is consumed east and north of those boundaries."

Southern Pacific 2-10-2 number 3672 hustles a block of Pacific Fruit Express reefers across the California landscape.

(Walter Dance, Morning Sun Books Collection)

REFRIGERATOR CARS

Why, one might ask, were there so many privately owned refrigerator cars and relatively few owned by the railroads themselves. Several factors influenced the railroads. The seasonal nature of shipments requiring protection from the heat or cold meant that the refrigerator cars would stand unused for periods of time. Private companies had a little more freedom to send the cars where needed. Probably the best example of private refrigerator car fleet utilization would be Fruit Growers Express, Burlington Refrigerator Express and Western Fruit Express. These three separate companies operated as one company. Cars of any one of the three companies could be found moving citrus fruit from Florida to the north at one time, moving potatoes from Idaho at another and moving produce out of the Midwest at others times.

Another reason that railroads didn't care to own too many refrigerator cars was their greater initial cost. Refrigerator cars simply cost more to build than a similar size box car. And refrigerator cars often returned empty from whence they came. There's no profit for the railroad in that. Railroads preferred cars that could be loaded both directions. Private companies were less adverse to owning cars if it meant that they could have tighter control over their car supply.

In 1941 the private car companies with the ten largest fleets were:

The fleets of General American, Union Tank Car and Sinclair were predominately tank cars. The other seven operated mainly refrigerator cars and, in 1941, practically all of these would have been ice bunker refrigerator cars.

OPERATION

There were two components to the operation of refrigerator cars, the cars themselves and protective services. The evolution of refrigerator cars may seem to have lagged behind that of box cars as wood ends, roofs and especially wood sides continued to be applied to refrigerator cars long after box cars were all steel. It was not because of backwardness on the part of the refrigerator car builders or owners but rather a belief that there was value in the extra insulating properties of wood when compared to steel. As better insulation became available wood was dropped in favor of steel because steel roofs, ends and sides required much less maintenance.

Private car companies generally provided their own protective services. Protective services consisted of pre-cooling, icing, re-icing and heating refrigerator cars as might be necessary. To pre-cool, the car's ice bunkers would be filled with ice sometime before loading. Cars might also be pre-cooled by having cool or cold air blown through the car usually by means of some arrangement of flexible ducts.

COMPANIES	CARS
General American Transportation Corp.	55,000
Union Tank Car Co.	39,000
Pacific Fruit Express Co.	36,030
Fruit Growers Express Co.	15,616
Merchants Despatch Transportation Corp.	13,139
American Refrigerator Transit Co.	9,962
Union Refrigerator Transit Lines	7,189
North American Car Corp.	7,151
Western Fruit Express Co.	7,010
Sinclair Refining Co.	6,468

Cars would be iced with chunk, coarse or crushed ice depending upon the commodity being carried and the desired temperature within the car. Chunk ice would be pieces not exceeding 100 pounds. Often skilled workmen would be able to break the 300 pound ice cakes into thirds or quarters just before the moving ice dropped into the bunker. Coarse ice consisted of pieces ranging in size from 10 to 20 pounds or thereabouts. Crushed ice, which was either prepared in advance or crushed mechanically would be about the size of a man's fist.

When additional ice was placed in a refrigerator car bunker it was necessary for the icing facility personnel to know in advance the commodity carried in the car or to have other instructions in order to place the proper size and amount of ice in the car and to add, if necessary, the correct proportion of salt.

Brine Spout in Open Position, Photographed from Two Perspectives.

Salt was added to speed the melting of the ice so as to achieve a lower temperature inside the car. Higher concentrations of salt required tanks to hold the brine. Originally the brine was just allowed to drip out of the refrigerator cars but when it became apparent that brine damaged track, bridges and the trucks of the refrigerator car, it became a requirement to hold brine within the car until such time as it could be drained at a location with proper facilities.

Some of the captions to come mention half-stage icing. When less than a full bunker of ice was required some cars were equipped with folding or collapsible grates that could be positioned so that only the top half of the bunker was filled with ice. Filling the top half of the bunker was more effective than filling the bottom half simply because the cold air circulation inside the car was improved.

In the years following World War Two air circulating fans, usually powered by one of the cars axles, were added to many refrigerator cars to improve the circulation. These fans were usually provided with other means to power the fan if the car was stationary for longer periods of time. There will be more on this in some of the captions to follow.

Some commodities such as lettuce required a layer of shaved ice be blown over the surface of the load. This was normally accomplished with some sort of mechanical device which both reduced the ice to flakes and blew it into place. There might be the necessity to replenish this so-called top or body ice en route. This, of course, had to be accomplished through the car doors rather than through the hatches in the roof.

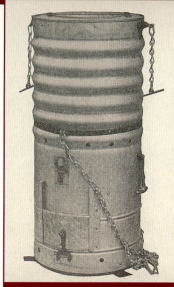

Charcoal Heater.

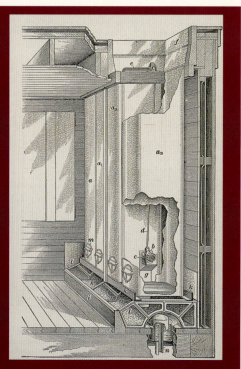

Brine Tanks Circa 1925.

Preco Fan Drive on Wheel.

Heaters were sometimes required to keep commodities from damage by freezing. Potatoes may be the most significant example of such a commodity that, in winter, required heaters. The earliest heaters burned oil or charcoal as fuel. The charcoal heaters had to be lighted and extinguished to maintain the desired temperatures. After World War Two alcohol heaters began to replace the charcoal heaters. Alcohol heaters had thermostats, could better maintain the desired temperature and needed little or no attention en route.

Heaters, one or two depending upon the outside temperature and the required inside temperature, were placed inside the car to the right of the door opening or, more typically in diagonally opposite ice bunkers. Any car with heaters required placards on both sides to warn of the possible toxic fumes inside. Before entering the car a certain amount of ventilation was required. Stories abound of workers losing consciousness inside the bunker when trying to remove or re-light the heaters.

Heaters could be owned by the shipper, private car company or railroad but in any case were not part of the car. In some cases the heaters of the delivering railroad were removed and replaced with those of the receiving railroad as was the case in Minneapolis, Minnesota where Great Northern or Northern Pacific heaters were removed and replaced with Chicago & North Western heaters before the cars were forwarded to Chicago. The Illinois Central (IC) and Minneapolis & St. Louis (M&StL), on the other hand, handled heaters through from Minneapolis to Chicago even though the M&StL handed the cars over to the IC at Albert Lea.

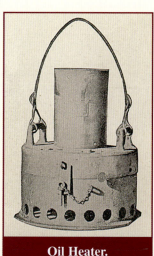

Oil Heater.

AAR MECHANICAL DESIGNATIONS

The Association of American Railroads developed a classification system of letters to identify the principal characteristics of freight and passenger cars. Most captions in this book include the mechanical designation. The mechanical designations changed from time to time as new car features were introduced and the use of older ones were discontinued. The AAR Mechanical Designations adopted in 1936 and 1952 are sufficient to describe all the cars in this book.

1936

BR – Refrigerator Express. An insulated car constructed and equipped for passenger train service, having ice bunkers or ice boxes. Designed primarily for use of chunk ice with means of ventilation and suitable to carry any perishable commodity requiring refrigeration or ventilation.

RA – Brine-Tank Refrigerator. A house car equipped with insulation and brine-tanks. Designed primarily for the combined use of crushed ice and salt usually without ventilating devices. Used chiefly for meats and packing house products.

RM – Beef Rail Refrigerator. A fully insulated house car equipped with either brine tanks or ice bunkers. Designed primarily for the combined use of crushed ice and salt usually and with or without means of ventilation. Equipped with beef rails and used chiefly for fresh meat and packing house products.

RS – Bunker Refrigerator. A fully insulated house car equipped with ice bunkers. Designed primarily for use of chunk ice and with or without means of ventilation.

1952

In 1952 the definition for "RM" was replaced by definitions "RA" and "RAM" and the definition "RSM" was added.

BR – Refrigerator Express. An insulated car constructed and equipped for passenger train service, having ice bunkers or ice boxes. Designed primarily for use of chunk ice with means of ventilation and suitable to carry any perishable commodity requiring refrigeration or ventilation.

RA – Brine-Tank Refrigerator. A house car equipped with insulation and brine-tanks. Designed primarily for the combined use of crushed ice and salt and usually without ventilating devices. Used chiefly for meats and packing house products.

RAM – Brine-Tank Refrigerator, similar to "RA" but equipped with beef rails

RS – Bunker Refrigerator. A fully insulated house car equipped with ice bunkers. Designed primarily for use of chunk ice and with or without means of ventilation.

RSM – Bunker Refrigerator, similar to "RS" but equipped with beef rails.

Let's start with what may be the oldest private owner, ice bunker refrigerator car in this book. New York Despatch Refrigerator Line's NYDX 15147 (RS), series 15000 through 15249, was added to the *Official Railway Equipment Register* sometime after March 1923 and before August 1923. The exact date this car was built remains elusive. New York Despatch Refrigerator Line was part of the Chicago, New York & Boston Refrigerator Line which was associated with the Grand Trunk Railway (later Grand Trunk Western Railway). With an overall length of 38 feet, 2 7/8 inches this car would have been typical of cars constructed during the early 1920s. This car has a steel underframe, a superstructure of mostly wood, ice tanks and insulation but was equipped with a door five feet wide. A door more typical for the time would have been four feet wide. The car was originally intended for the transportation of dairy products but to what use it was later put is unknown. The car is now equipped with the AB air brake system and modern cast sideframe trucks but, when new, would have had a K system air brake and probably arch bar trucks although we can't be sure about the trucks. This photo was taken in Barre, Massachusetts sometime in the late 1940s which also makes this view one of the oldest photographs to be shown in this book. *(Arthur E. Mitchell)*

ICING REFRIGERATOR CARS

The following series of photographs was taken at the 20th Street icing stage in Columbus, Ohio in June 1962. Recognizing he was witnessing a vanishing art and part of railroading's landscape hardly photographed, the late Paul Winters set out to record these rare scenes. The steps depicted here were typical at many other points in the United States of re-icing a string of reefers.

Left • All is ready in anticipation of the arrival of a string of reefers. *(All photos page 6-9, Paul C. Winters)*

Below • The reefers arrive with URTX 67310 in the foreground.

Below • First, the ice hatches are opened.

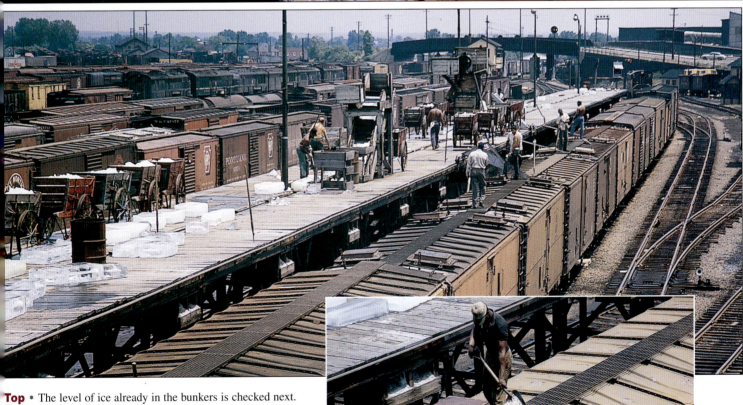

Top • The level of ice already in the bunkers is checked next.

Center • Ice is added to bring the level in the bunkers to the proper level for the commodity being carried. In the foreground is PFE mechanical reefer 300344.

Right • Salt is added to the bunkers of URTX 67310.

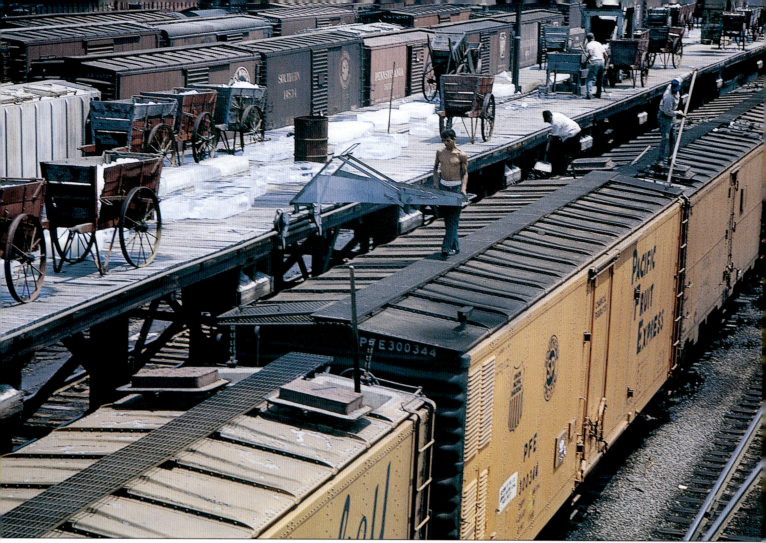

Above and Below • The chute is being walked across the top of PFE mechanical reefer 300344 and is placed in position to put crushed ice into the bunkers of URTX 67310.

Above • Crushed ice is chuted into the bunkers of URTX 67310.

Left • Excess ice is shoveled off the top.

Right • Salt has been added to the bunker and the salt/ice combination is being tamped prior to closing the hatches. Tamping fills any voids in the ice and mixes the salt and ice.

ICING FACILITIES

Below • Icing facilities were unique, expensive structures that stood out in any rail yard. While similarities exist, here are several examples in different parts of the country using different approaches. This and the next two photos show a broader view of the facilities and equipment at the 20th Street icing stage, Columbus, Ohio, November 21, 1962. *(Paul C. Winters)*

Right • Refrigerator cars being iced in the distance at 20th Street icing stage, Columbus, Ohio, May 20, 1962. *(Paul C. Winters)*

Top • Ice being skidded on planks into the bunkers at 20th Street icing stage, Columbus, Ohio, May 20, 1962. *(Paul C. Winters)*

Center • Reefers, including MDT 12530, are being re-iced from a truck in the Virginian Railway Yards, Norfolk, Virginia on April 10, 1955. Instructions on the car side direct that the car be returned to the GM&O in Mobile, Alabama when empty.*(Russ.F. Munroe)*

Right • The front half of the cargo bed of the truck is lifted by a hydraulic cylinder to bring the ice to the car's roof top. This scene is along 19th Street, Mason City, Iowa on February 20, 1962. NWX #613 is on the electrified Iowa Terminal. *(Soph Marty)*

Right • This view shows the Milwaukee Road yards in Austin, Minnesota where Hormel had a packing plant. The date is August 1969. *(Jerry Hesley)*

Below • Milwaukee Road yards, Austin, Minnesota, October 1972. *(Jerry Hesley)*

Right • As if to prove that automation came to refrigerator car icing at an early date we see the Clinchfield Railroad ice machine in Erwin, Tennessee on July 18, 1956. *(G. M Leilich)*

Right • Boston & Maine's mechanical icing machine at Mechanicville, New York, October 30, 1965.
(Russell F. Munroe)

Below • Norfolk & Western's East Portsmouth Yard, Portsmouth, Ohio, August 4, 1962. A string of reefers is being shoved from the right to the icing stage.
(Paul C. Winters)

Left • Refrigerator cars from four meat packers, from left to right Hormel, Morrell, Wilson and Armour, are about to be iced at East Portsmouth Yard, August 4, 1962.
(Paul C. Winters)

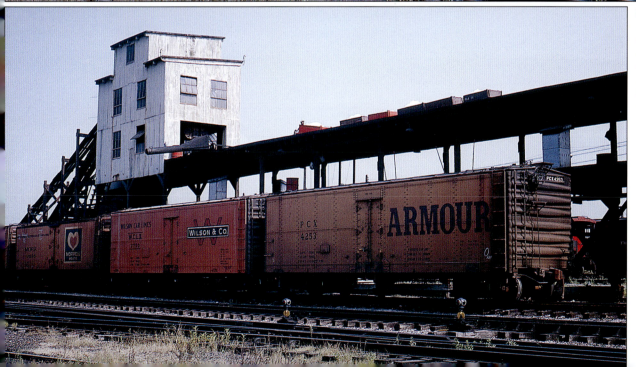

AMERICAN REFRIGERATOR TRANSIT COMPANY

American Refrigerator Transit (ART) was formed in the late 19th Century by two railroads controlled by Jay Gould, the Wabash and Missouri Pacific, to supply refrigerator cars for those lines. ART was an early user of all steel refrigerator cars. The first were copied from PFE's R-40-10 refrigerator cars and were delivered in 1936.

Eventually ART also entered the leasing business. ART, now headquartered in Omaha, Nebraska, continues in the car leasing business but refrigerator cars are no longer among the less than 200 cars on the ART roster.

Above • Series 50000 through 50999 first appeared in 1954 suggesting that these cars were rebuilt from cars built earlier. The dimensions of the 50000 series reefers match those of the 17000 through 19999 series. When rebuilt, cars such as ART 50393, seen here on February 12, 1964, received air circulating fans. This paint scheme is not typical. The Wabash and MoPac heralds are missing from the right side. *(Richard Zmijewski)*

Below • This is an example of refrigerator car construction typical of the 1920s and early 1930s having been built by the Pressed Steel Car Company at their Hegewisch (Chicago) facility in 1928. Builders continued to use wood exteriors for the insulating properties of wood. ART 52941, seen here in January 1955, was rebuilt in November 1954 hence the fresh paint and general good condition. Cars in series 21000 through 21999 were renumbered to the 52000 series as they were rebuilt. *(Emery J. Gulash, Morning Sun Books collection)*

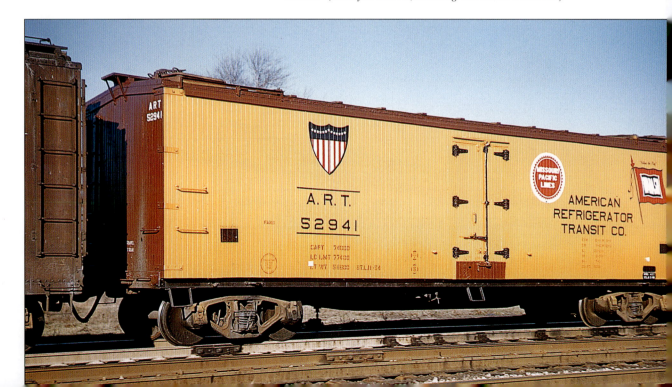

Right • All-steel cars in series 24000 through 24999 were built in late 1939 by American Refrigerator Transit in their St. Louis company shops from kits supplied by American Car & Foundry. ART 24582, seen here in Camden, New Jersey on April 3, 1954, is one of the earliest examples of a refrigerator car with the 4-panel sides and horizontal riveted seams. The electric locomotives are PRR E2b 4944 and P5a 4707.
(Frank C. Kozempel)

Above and Below • Both sides of ART 27398 (above and below) were photographed in February 1949 to show an earlier paint scheme on series 27100 through 27999. This series was built in May, June and July 1948 by General American. Notice the use of 3-color company heralds. Economy would bring simplification to one color eventually. The cars in this series were equipped for stage icing and had air circulating fans.
(Both photos, Carl Solheim collection)

Right • ART 29137, built in August, was one of 500 cars in the series 29000 through 29499 built by Mount Vernon Car Mfg. Div. of Pressed Steel Car Co. for ART in 1952. These were regular ice bunker reefers with no meat rails. In this scene in the Milwaukee yard, Mason City, Iowa, it is January 24, 1971. *(Soph Marty)*

Below • ART 31071 was part of series of reefers numbered 31000 through 31999 built by American Car and Foundry and General American Transportation Corp. This example was built in December 1936, equipped with air circulating fans and was set up for stage icing whereby dividers could be raised in the ice bunkers to allow only the top half of the bunker to be loaded with ice. This shot was taken in Council Bluffs, Iowa on February 20, 1965. *(Lou Schmitz)*

Right • ART 31283 and the other reefers of series 31000 through 31999, were originally built in December 1936 and numbered in series 22979-23999. They were quite modern for their time. This car appears to be freshly painted as seen here in August 1960 in Columbus, Ohio.
(Dick Argo)

Above • Old reefers never die. They just get put in ice service. ART 36142 was built in December 1936, originally numbered in the 2979-23999 series, and is seen here in Irving, Texas in November 1971. Ice service cars transport ice from point of production to point of use. *(Ed Stoll, Lloyd Keyser collection)*

Below • American Refrigerator Transit built 300 cars in series 26000 through 26299 in their own shops. ART 26274 (RS) was built in September 1947 and was still in service in May 1995 when this photo was taken. *(Rail Data Services collection)*

Right • Ice hatch covers were sometimes fixed in an open position to provide ventilation as seen here on ART 26281 in Dallas, Texas in March 1971.
(Ed Stoll, Lloyd Keyser collection)

Below • ART 27587, built in August 1948 by General American was photographed in the L&N yard, Huntsville, Alabama in February 1971. This car was part of series 27100 through 27999, had circulating fans and was equipped for stage icing, right side view L&N Yard, Huntsville, Alabama.
(Bernie Wooller)

Below • When the Wabash became part of the Norfolk & Western in the mid-1960s the Wabash flag herald began to be replaced by the N&W logo. Pullman-Standard built series 28000 through 28899 including ART 28076 in September 1947 and seen here in Endicott, NY in August 1969.
(Rail Data Services collection)

Right • Compare ART 28387, seen here in February 1994, with the preceding photograph of sister car ART 28076 to compare the old paint scheme with the new. Pullman-Standard (P-S) built cars 28000 through 28899 for ART as P-S Lot 5878 beginning in September 1947.
(The Houser collection)

Left • The cars in series 31000 through 31999, built by ACF and GATC, were renumbered from cars in the 22979-23999 series in the early 1950s as they were equipped with air circulating fans. This well lit view, taken in March of 1969, of ART 31157, built in December 1936, affords a good view of the details. Originally constructed in 1936, these cars were close copies of Pacific Fruit Express reefers in PFE class R-40-10.
(Ed Stoll, Lloyd Keyser collection)

Right • ART 37073, from series 37000 through 37249, was built in June 1957 by Pacific Car & Foundry. This car was in Huntsville, Alabama in January 1970.
(Bernie Wooller)

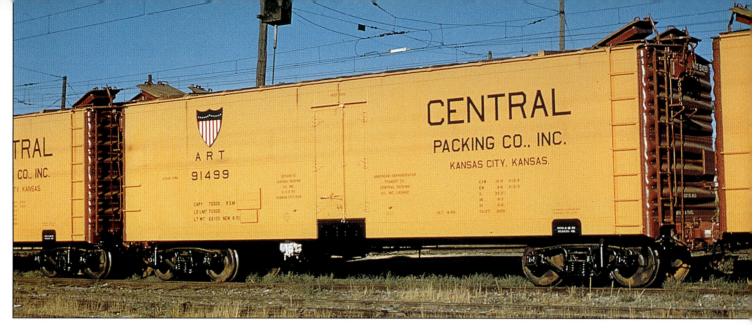

Above • American Refrigerator Transit rostered relatively few meat reefers but ART 91499, part of series 91300 through 91699, was equipped with meat rails. This car was built in August 1958 by PC&F and was photographed September 22, 1958 in Othello, Washington in the company of other new cars also lettered for Central Packing Co. Inc. in Kansas City, Kansas.
(Wade Stevenson)

Below • ART 91501 was built by Pacific Car & Foundry in July 1958 as part of series 91300 through 91699. Most ART reefers were simply ice bunker reefers, mechanical designation RS but this series was equipped with meat rails for handling entire slabs of meat on hooks. The car is stenciled "ASSIGNED CAR RETURN REVERSE ROUTE AGENT KCS RY NEOSHO, MO." This shot was taken in Huntsville, Alabama in July 1969. Compare this car to ART 91519 in the next photo to see what the paint looked like when new. *(Bernie Wooller)*

Right • ART 91519, photographed at an unknown location in September 1962, shows that not all cars in series 91300 through 91699 were lettered for meat packers. This car was built in July 1958 by PC&F.
(Rail Data Services collection)

Right • Some cars from series 91300 through 91699, such as ART 91687, built August 1958 by PC&F, seen here in Othello, Washington, September 27, 1958, were lettered for Royal Packing Company. These cars were equipped with Ajax hand brakes.
(Wade Stevenson)

Left • ART 91695, stenciled "RETURN EMPTY TO TRRA EAST ST LOUIS ILLINOIS," is in Othello, Washington on September 27, 1958. This car was built in August 1958 by PC&F.
(Wade Stevenson)

Below • This photo shows the effect of weather and service on ART 91697 and ART 91699 after about 35 years of use. These cars are part of series 91300 through 91699 built by PC&F and seen here in St. Louis, Missouri in July 1993.
(The Houser collection)

ARMOUR COMPANY

Philip Danforth Armour (1832-1901) founded the meat packing business that bore his name on Archer Road in Chicago in 1867. The term "meat packing" stems from packing pork in salt and brine in barrels. Beef was not eaten in great quantities until after the US Civil War. By 1925 Armour and Company operated plants in all the major meat packing centers (in order of size of the Armour facility) including Chicago, Illinois; Kansas City, Kansas; South Omaha, Nebraska; East St. Louis, Illinois; South St. Paul, Minnesota; Ft. Worth, Texas; St. Joeseph, Missouri; Sioux City, Iowa; New York, New York; and Denver, Colorado as well as eight smaller facilities. Armour also operates 400 "branch houses" where meat was cut and packaged for retail sale.

For almost 100 years meat packers followed the same business model until the formation of Iowa Beef Packers (IBP) in 1960. (More about IBP in another section.) Livestock - cattle, hogs, sheep, lambs and veal calves - were slaughtered at locations near the livestock producers. Trimmed and cooled carcasses are then shipped to branch houses, mostly in refrigerator cars, where the meat is packaged for the consumer or local retailer. As an outgrowth of providing refrigerator cars for its business, Armour began to provide refrigerator cars for transportation of fruit, vegetables and produce as well as meat for other packers. Armour's refrigerator fleet and the attendant icing facilities grew to such an extent that Armour was able to extract rebates from the railroads and charge exorbitant prices to ice refrigerator cars. In 1920, based on legal actions begun earlier, Armour was required to divest itself of more than half of its reefer fleet as well as other parts of Armour & Co. not related to meat packing.

Armour's car fleet during the 1920s, 1930s and 1940s hovered around 5000 cars with a high over 6000 in 1931 and a low of just under 3300 in 1948. In 1954 the fleet was steady at about 3200 cars but by 1963 the count was down to 625 due to changes in the meat packing industry on the one hand and leasing cars instead of owning them on the other. Even when the leased cars are included the total is less than 1600 cars. Armour & Co. continued to add facilities in various parts of the United States during the 1930s and 1940s. By 1953 the first meat packers moved out of Chicago to be closer to the supply of livestock and by 1960 the last meat packer left. The character of the meat packing industry changed and transportation of meat by rail began to shrink.

Greyhound acquired Armour in 1970, and by 1973 Armour's fleet was a mere 4 refrigerator cars bearing ARLX reporting marks. Armour & Company's history beyond that point is outside the scope of this book.

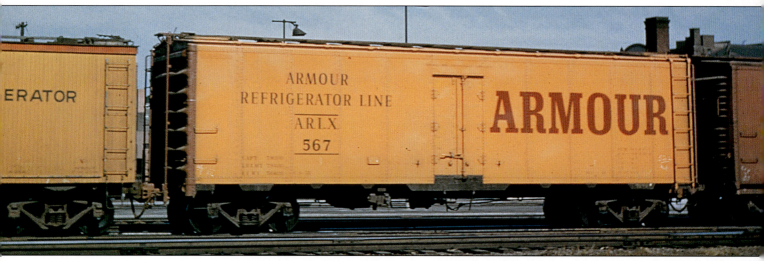

Above • Armour meat reefer (AAR mechanical designation RAM) ARLX 567 was one of a group, numbered 1 to 2000, built by General American Transportation (GATC) in 1948 and 1949. Some of this group of cars were rebuilt by Pacific Car and Foundry (PCF) in 1956. This reefer was found in Omaha, Nebraska on October 10, 1953 *(Lou Schmitz)*

Below • Armour's ARLX 607 is another meat reefer from the series 1 to 2000 which was built in February 1949 by GATC. This car is in Othello, Washington on May 30, 1956. Judging by the new paint it may be fresh from rebuilding by PCF. *(Wade Stevenson)*

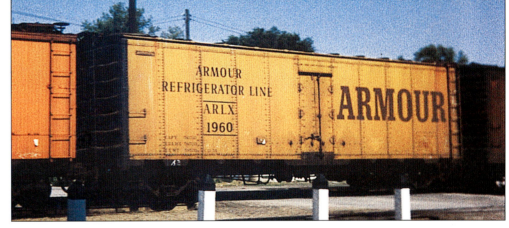

Above • This in service photo shows ARLX 1574 in Tampa, Florida some time in the mid-1950s judging by the automobiles barely visible under this meat reefer. This car was built in January 1949 by GATC.
(K.B. King, Jr., Lloyd Keyser collection)

Right • In September 1955 ARLX 1960 is in Lawrence, Kansas. The AAR mechanical designation for these cars in Armour's series 1 to 2000 was RAM. "R" stands for refrigerator car, "A" indicates the car is equipped with brine tanks, and "M" is added for cars which have meat rails for carrying large slabs of meat on hooks.
(Don Ball)

Below • Armour leased the cars in series 4000 to 4399 from Packers Car Line, hence the reporting marks PCX. (Reporting marks were recycled, too. As recently as 1942 PCX reporting marks were used by the Pittsburgh Coal Carbonization Company.) Car number 4190 was built by PCF in August 1957 and is seen here in Othello, Washington on September 8, 1957 in a string of brand new cars ready for delivery to Armour. This car's mechanical designation is RSM which means that instead of brine tanks the cars is equipped with ice bunkers. The car on the right is TRAX 13004. *(Wade Stevenson)*

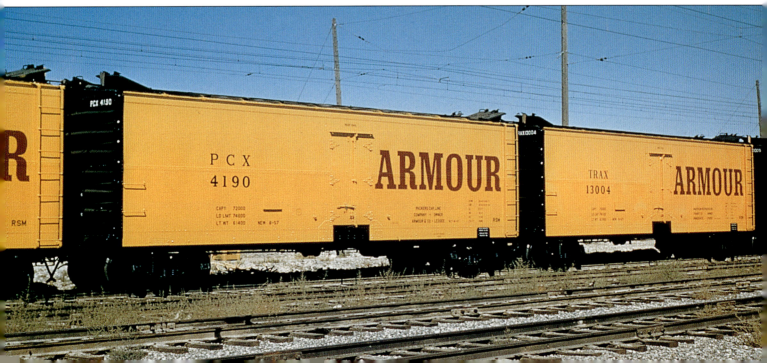

Right • Packers Car Line 4243 and 67 other equally new reefers for lease to Armour stretch off into the distance in Othello, Washington on September 8, 1957. These cars, built by Pacific Car and Foundry, were assigned to PCX series 4000 to 4399. *(Wade Stevenson)*

Below • Packers Car Line car number 4408 was built in June 1957. This car has ice bunkers and meat rails making it an RSM. By July 3, 1980, the date of this, the ladders have been shortened and the running board has been removed to comply with the latest AAR regulations for interchange. The horizontal seam design feature, which will be seen often in this book, reduced the number of seams in the car side. This design have only four pieces of sheet steel in the side can be traced back at least to late 1939, according to Ed Hawkins, when American Refrigerator Transit (ART) built cars in series 24000-24099 in their St. Louis company shops. American Car and Foundry (ACF) supplied "kits" from which ART built the cars. Cars using the horizontal seam feature were also built by ACF, GATC and PCF as well as ART. PCF built this car. *(Randy Garnhart)*

Below • Armour leased PCX 4460 from Packers Car Line. This car was built in August 1957 and is seen here in Council Bluffs, Iowa on January 15, 1967. *(Lou Schmitz)*

Left • PCX 4203 was built by Pacific Car and Foundry in August 1957. The lettering above the door says "MEAT RAIL." Armour operated a packing plant, the former Jacob E. Decker facility, in Mason City, Iowa until the early 1970s. This car is in the former M&StL yard in Mason City on June 22, 1970. The C&NW took over M&StL in 1960.
(Soph Marty)

Below • Armour leased the cars in series 12000 through 12599 from American Refrigerator Transit. TRAX 12021, built in May 1954 by Pacific Car and Foundry, has brine tanks and meat rails. The car is relatively new in this shot taken in 1955 at an unrecorded location.
(K.B. King, Jr., Lloyd Keyser collection)

Right • TRAX 12346 from series 12000 through 12599 is passing through Lawrence, Kansas in April 1956. This car, owned by American Refrigerator Transit (ART) and leased by Armour, was built in June 1954 by PCF. This car has the mechanical designation RAM which means it has brine tanks and meat rails. *(Don Ball)*

Right • This nearly new car was photographed in Othello, Washington August 7, 1954. TRAX 12415 was one of the cars in series 12000 through 12599 built by PCF in June 1954. ART owned these cars and leased them to Armour.
(Wade Stevenson)

Above • Pacific Car and Foundry built this car in July 1954 for ART which leased it to Armour. TRAX 12427 is seen here August 7 1954 in Othello, Washington.
(Wade Stevenson)

Below • Brand new TRAX 13001 was the second car in series 13000 through 13014 which was built by PCF in September 1957. The mechanical designation RSM indicates that this car, seen here in Othello, Washington September 8, 1957, has ice bunkers and meat rails. Armour leased this car series from American Refrigerator Transit. *(Wade Stevenson)*

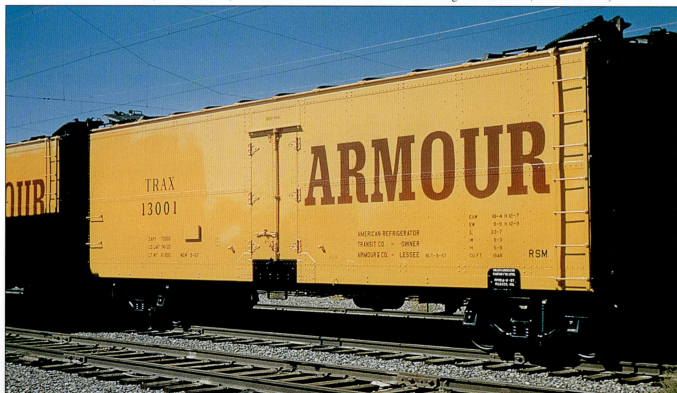

CUDAHY CAR LINES
OWNED AND OPERATED BY
THE CUDAHY PACKING COMPANY
Chicago, Illinois

In 1892 Patrick and John Cudahy [kud´uhE´´] founded the Cudahy meat packing firm in what was to become Cudahy, Wisconsin. Patrick Cudahy was able to persuade the Chicago & North Western to create a stop at a point where Cudahy bought 700 acres along Lake Michigan, most of which was to be the site of the packing plant and the remainder was laid out in lots for homes of the workers.

The Cudahy Packing Company owned and operated Cudahy Car Lines to provide the needed refrigerator cars for the transportation of their products. In the late 1930s Cudahy also leased refrigerator cars numbered between 1001 through 1250 from Mather. The Mather leases ended before 1942. Cudahy leased refrigerator cars numbered 1501 through 2000 from 1942 until the end of operations in the 1960s. Refrigerator cars leased from either Mather or General American always bore CRLX reporting marks. The size of the Cudahy refrigerator car fleet ranged from nearly 2000 in the late 1920s to about 1000 in the late 1940s and early 1950s. In the 1960s the fleet dwindled to zero by 1966.

Above • This beautiful shot was taken in Shreveport, Louisiana in 1959 and Cudahy's refrigerator car CRLX 6766 (RSM) stand out prominently in the foreground. All Cudahy reefers had meat rails so we might suppose this car is loaded with hanging sides of beef, pork or mutton for delivery to a local branch facility where the sides of meat will be cut and wrapped for sale at the local grocery stores. Notice the short KCS/L&A passenger train on the third track from the right. *(David H. Hickcox)*

Above • CRLX 5802 (RSM), series 5701 through 5850, was photograph in May 1961 at an unknown location. The number series 5701-5850 first appeared in the mid-1940s but it is not clear whether these were new cars or renumbered cars. These cars were equipped with National Type B-1 trucks which can be easily recognized by the two round holes directly below the springs in each side frame. *(Rail Data Services collection)*

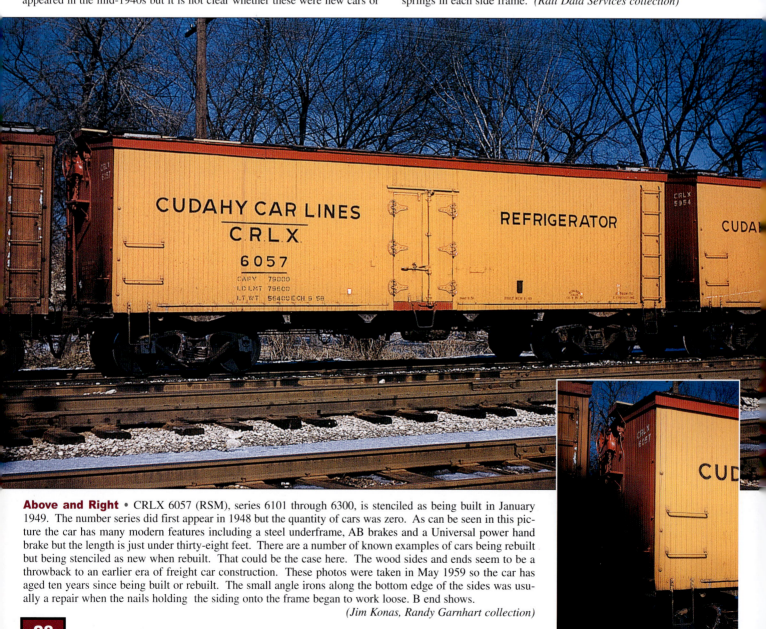

Above and Right • CRLX 6057 (RSM), series 6101 through 6300, is stenciled as being built in January 1949. The number series did first appear in 1948 but the quantity of cars was zero. As can be seen in this picture the car has many modern features including a steel underframe, AB brakes and a Universal power hand brake but the length is just under thirty-eight feet. There are a number of known examples of cars being rebuilt but being stenciled as new when rebuilt. That could be the case here. The wood sides and ends seem to be a throwback to an earlier era of freight car construction. These photos were taken in May 1959 so the car has aged ten years since being built or rebuilt. The small angle irons along the bottom edge of the sides was usually a repair when the nails holding the siding onto the frame began to work loose. B end shows.

(Jim Konas, Randy Garnhart collection)

Above • Cudahy's refrigerator car CRLX 6067 (RSM), series 6101 through 6300, was built in January 1949 according to information stenciled on the side. The car has an overall length of less that thirty-eight feet and is of a style of construction more typical of the 1920s than the 1940s. Perhaps the car was rebuilt in 1949. This shot dates from 1957 in Tampa, Florida.

(K. B. King, Jr., Lloyd Keyser collection)

Below • We conclude our look at Cuddly refrigerator cars with this shot showing the juxtaposition of the old and the new. CRUX 6270 (RSV), series 6101 through 6300, with wood sides and ends is shown adjacent to an Illinois Central piggyback trailer loaded on a flat car. The running board on top of CRUX 6270 is from Morton - note the round holes in the running board - which was first approved for use effective January 1, 1944. This overhead shot was taken in 1963 in Binghamton, New York.

(Chuck Yungkurth, Rail Data Services collection)

FRUIT GROWERS EXPRESS COMPANY
Washington, D. C.

BURLINGTON REFRIGERATOR EXPRESS COMPANY
Washington, D. C.

WESTERN FRUIT EXPRESS COMPANY
Washington, D. C.

Fruit Growers Express, Burlington Refrigerator Express and Western Fruit Express operated as one company. The principal officers of all three companies were the same people and the three companies shared some of the refrigerator car designs. For these reasons we will look at these three companies together in this section.

Fruit Growers Express, using the reporting marks FGEX, had its beginning in 1920 when it obtained a little over 4000 refrigerator cars as well as shops in Alexandria, Virginia and Jacksonville, Florida from the Armour fleet which had been broken up by the Federal Trade Commission the previous year. Railroads initially owning FGEX were the Southern, Atlantic Coast Line, Baltimore & Ohio and the Pennsylvania. The New Haven and Norfolk and Western soon joined the first four. The B&O's cars weren't added to the fleet until May 15, 1925.

In 1923 the Great Northern Railway formed Western Fruit Express (WFEX) for the purpose of pooling cars with Fruit Growers Express. Offices and officers of WFEX were the same as those of FGEX which had been dependent upon seasonal harvests in Southern States and therefore had idle cars at certain times of the year. In the Pacific Northwest the harvest of berries, fruit and potatoes took place at a different time. By pooling their resources the combined companies could own fewer cars but keep them busy more of the time.

In 1926 the Burlington Refrigerator Express (BREX) was formed by the Chicago, Burlington & Quincy and again the offices and officers are the same as FGEX.

The Chesapeake & Ohio joined in 1927, the New York, Ontario & Western in 1931. Eventually the Central of Georgia, the Chicago & Eastern Illinois, the Florida East Coast, the Louisville & Nashville, the Richmond, Fredericksburg & Potomac and the Seaboard Air Line would all be part owners of Fruit Growers Express.

Meanwhile, in 1928, National Car Company (NX) was formed as a subsidiary of FGEX to serve meat packers such as Kahns (EKSX) and Rath (RPRX). About 1950 National Car also had reefers with MNX reporting marks.

FGEX WOOD REEFERS

Above • FGEX 34444 is representative of one of FGEX's own designs which first appeared about 1923 as series 32100 through 33099, later extended to 35999. This car was photographed June 15, 1980 in Cincinnati, Ohio. *(Emery J. Gulash, Morning Sun Books collection)*

Above • This shot shows some of the details of the end and hand brake on FGEX 34444 while the car was in Cincinnati, Ohio in September 1979. *(Dick Argo)*

Above • FGEX 37845, from series 36000 through 37999, is an example of cars built at East Chicago, Indiana during 1928 by FGEX on an underframe of their own design. Western Fruit Express (WFEX) also had cars of this design. This car was located in Enola, Pennsylvania in January 1978. A few details are different than the as-built car suggesting at least one rebuilding. Originally the right half of the side would have carried the lettering 'VENTILATOR AND REFRIGERATOR." *(H.E. Brouse)*

Right and Below • When Fruit Growers Express was first formed, aside from the initial group of cars from Armour, the FGEX fleet was made up of cars contributed by the roads which joined FGEX. The Pennsylvania Railroad, effective May 1, 1922, added almost 3000 cars from their class R7 to the FGEX fleet. FGEX 45216, seen here in Jersey City, New Jersey in November 1960, is an example one of the cars which were assigned to FGEX series 43500 through 46799. This design was exclusive to the Pennsylvania Railroad which used it on both box and refrigerator cars.

(Both, K.B. King, Jr., Lloyd Keyser collection)

Right • Well weathered FGEX 55558 stands in Wildwood, Florida November 12, 1981. This car, part of series 55000 through 58899, was rebuilt in the Jacksonville shops in August 1948 where it was, among other changes and improvements, equipped with a Universal 2050 power hand brake.
(Emery J. Gulash, Morning Sun Books collection)

Above • This car, FGEX 56075, was rebuilt in November 1948 and has been given a new light weight in January 1955 so this clipped photo at an unknown location was taken in 1955 or later. *(K.B. King, Jr., Lloyd Keyser collection)*

Below • Cars in ICE SERVICE wore plain Jane paint as seen here on FGEX 56432 in January 1973 on the Denver & Rio Grande Western in Alamosa, Colorado. *(Lloyd Keyser collection)*

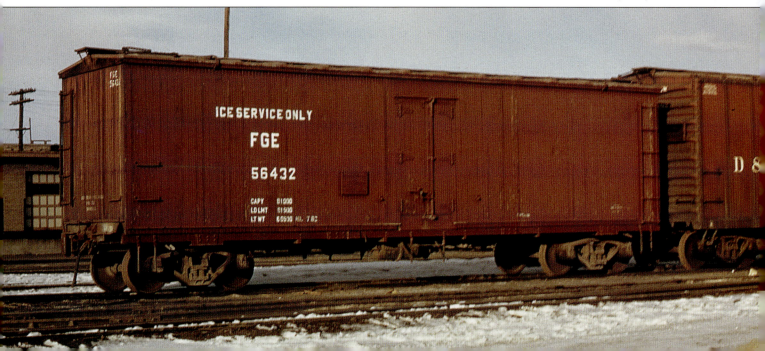

Above • FGEX 56525, part of series 55000 through 58899 was rebuilt in October 1950 and was photographed in Washington, DC in February 1970, almost 20 years later. Apparently as cars from other series were rebuilt beginning in 1947 they were renumbered into this series.
(Jim Rogers)

Below • When rebuilt in Atlanta in October 1947 this car was renumbered FGEX 57092 as part of series 55000 through 58899. Again we see a Universal 2050 power hand brake. Details varied from car to car in this group. Compare the square-cornered gusset on the end of the body bolster with the angled gusset on the car in the preceding photo. The car is in Dallas, Texas in March 1970.
(Lloyd Keyser collection)

Right • On September 5, 1976, well weathered FGEX 57266 was in Williard, Ohio. The paint is so weathered here that not much can be learned about the car from the lettering but the power hand brake, Universal again, suggests rebuilding. *(Bob Jetmore, Bob Wilt collection)*

Above • This car was rebuilt in 1948 by Fruit Growers Express and most recently reweighed in June 1969. FGEX 57513 is seen here in Huntsville, Alabama. *(Bernie Wooller)*

Below • When rebuilt by FGEX in August 1948 this car received air circulating fans. Apparently not all of the diverse cars rebuilt and renumbered into series 55000 through 58899 were equipped with fans. Notice the flange like bracket on the bottom of the side of FGEX 57607 just above the left truck. This is part of the fan mechanism. The date is March 7, 1970. The place is Council Bluffs, Iowa and the car was repainted in 1969. *(Lou Schmitz)*

Right • More than 2200 cars from this series were still in service when FGEX 57826 (RS), series 57000 through 57899, was photographed in Altoona, Pennsylvania May 9, 1974. The date rebuilt is no longer visible but the last reweigh, which may coincide with the last repainting is 1966. This car was equipped for stage icing. *(C.T. Bossler)*

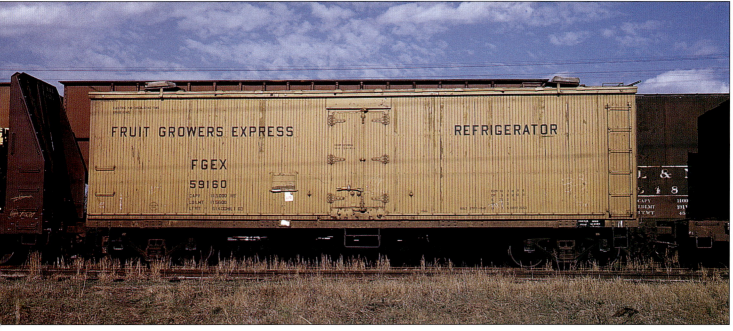

Above • FGEX 59160 (RS), series 59000 through 59999, was rebuilt in January 1948 and photographed at Huntsville, Alabama in March 1967. The 57000 and 59000 series had identical dimensions but different capacities. Cars in the 57000 series had a capacity of 75,000 pounds while cars in the 59000 series had a capacity of 90,000 pounds. The usual reason for such differences in capacities would be differences in trucks. *(Bernie Wooller)*

Below • FGEX 59531 was a member of series 59000 through 59899 which were cars renumbered into this series when rebuilt beginning in 1948. The car is in Dallas, Texas on march 1969. *(Lloyd Keyser collection)*

Above • FGEX 59999 was rebuilt by FGEX at the Jacksonville, Florida shops in 1954. Some cars were equipped for stage icing or received air circulating fans. This one received both. The car is at the end of its useful life in Cincinnati, Ohio on June 15, 1980. *(Emery J. Gulash, Morning Sun Books collection)*

FOBX OVERHEAD ICE BUNKERS

Below • Fruit Growers Express had, beginning about 1940 with FGEX 600, a number of cars in three series that had overhead ice bunkers, were 55 feet long and had an interior length of 50 feet making them somewhat unusual in appearance. These cars carried FOBX reporting marks (OB=overhead bunkers). FOBX 736, part of series 700 through 773, is in Reading, Pennsylvania on May 30, 1969. *(C.T. Bossler)*

Above • The third series of overhead bunker reefers, built in FGEX company shops, was FGEX 4000 through 4174 to which series FOBX 4126 belonged. These cars were equipped with ice bunkers, not brine tanks. Notice that the ladders and grab irons are let into the sides to stay within the clearance diagram and still provide the required clearance around the rungs for safety. This car is in Dallas, Texas in March 1967. *(Lloyd Keyser collection)*

FGEX STEEL REEFERS

Left • At the same time that FGEX was rebuilding many of the wood-sheathed cars in its fleet FGEX also began to acquire all-steel ice bunker refrigerator cars such as FGEX 38947, built August 1948, seen above in Cincinnati, Ohio in September 1979. These cars were equipped for stage icing and had electric air circulating fans. Collapsible end bulkheads allowed the entire interior length to be used for lading when icing was not required. *(Dick Argo)*

Left • Our photographer caught this view of FGEX 59783, during July 1971 in Dallas, Texas. This angle and the good lighting give us and excellent view of the Standard Improved Dreadnaught end and Universal hand brake. FGEX 59783 is one of a group of cars rebuilt by Pacific Car and Foundry in 1950. These cars were equipped with plug doors, air circulating fans and equipped for stage icing.

(Lloyd Keyser collection)

37

Right • FHIX 40557 was one of more than 900 cars built by Pacific Car and Foundry in 1957 and numbered in series 40000 through 40960. This July 1960 shot in Columbus, Ohio shows the car just over three years old.
(Dick Argo)

Below • Pacific Car and Foundry built this series (41241 through 41640) in 1957. FHIX 41475, seen here in August 1970, and the other cars in this series were equipped with electric air circulating fans, side wall flues, and stage icing. The letters "HI" in FHIX stood for "heavy insulation." *(Paul C. Winters)*

BURLINGTON REFRIGERATOR EXPRESS

Right • This is the only car design shared by FGEX, BREX and WFEX. All three companies received the first of these cars in 1942. World War Two was already in progress and steel was limited so the initial cars for all three companies had plywood sides including BREX's first 100 cars which were numbered in the series 74400 through 74699. When Burlington Refrigerator Express received more cars later during the war the sides were tongue and groove lumber as seen here on BREX 74458 in January 1961 at the CB&Q's Hawthorne yard in Cicero, Illinois.
(Chuck Yungkurth, Rail Data Services collection)

Above • The date built stenciled on the side of BREX 74203, photographed October 30 1953 in Othello, Washington, is September 1949 and the reweigh date is April 1953 which appears to be when this car was last painted. The 200 cars in series 74200 through 74399 were equipped for stage icing and, except for 74399, with Preco air circulating fans. Two cars, 74398 and 74399, had permanent underslung heaters. *(Wade Stevenson)*

Below • It is April 16, 1955 in Othello, Washington and we see BREX 74377 which was one of the cars in series 74200 through 74399 which were built in 1949 for Burlington Refrigerator Express. Note the different railroad slogans. *(Wade Stevenson)*

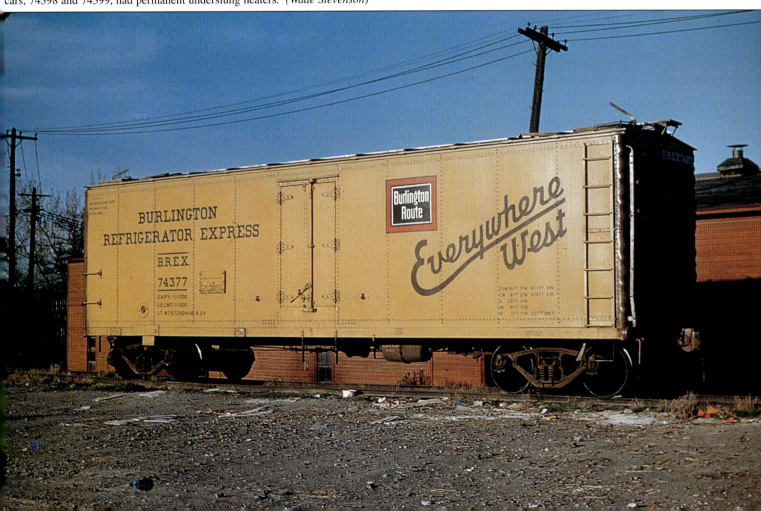

Right • Burlington Refrigerator Express 76060 was built in 1957 at FGE's Indiana harbor shops as part of series 76000 through 76249 and is seen here at Fort Worth, Texas in August 1970. The hand brake is from Universal.
(Ed Stoll, Lloyd Keyser collection)

Inset • This detail view from August 1970 of Burlington Refrigerator Express 76056 clearly shows external details of the air circulating fan. The round opening admits a pulley which can be driven by an electric motor when the car is not moving to keep air circulating. The bracket below is part of the apparatus that drive the fans when the car is in motion. A drive wheel rests against one of the cars wheels and drives the fans mechanically. *(Paul C. Winters)*

WESTERN FRUIT EXPRESS

Below • WFEX 60413 was part of series 60001 through 63910. Notice that this car has a truss-rod underframe, something unusual in the 1950s. Cars in this series were built for the Great Northern and were repainted for Western Fruit Express after the GN created WFEX. Sioux City, Iowa, where this shot was taken in September 1954, was one of the important meat packing centers in the Midwest with large plants from Armour, Cudahy and Swift. This car lacks meat rails and is more likely here to be unloaded. *(George Berkstresser, Lloyd Keyser collection)*

Above • As mentioned earlier in the BREX caption on page 38, FGEX, BREX and WFEX all received steel reefers with plywood sides in 1942 when steel was hard to get. WFEX 66422, seen here in February 1968, still has her plywood sides. The 100 cars in series 66400 through 66499 were built in 1942 without air circulating fans but received them later. *(Paul C. Winters)*

Below • Many, if not all, reefers from WFEX series 72000 through 72054, including WFEX 72019 seen here in Huntsville, Alabama in November 1964, were rebuilt by Pacific Car and Foundry in 1952. When rebuilt the cars were renumbered from another series. This car came out of rebuilding in June 1952. This car has the more traditional GN mountain goat logo as compared to the new image version in the photo above. *(Bernie Wooller)*

Above • Another series of WFEX reefers with wood sides and ends which were rebuilt by Pacific Car and Foundry were those numbered 72055 through 72179. WFEX 72123, photographed in Huntsville, Alabama in April 1966, was renumbered from some other series. The rebuilding program for these cars began in 1948. *(Bernie Wooller)*

Below • Another PCF rebuild is WFEX 72169 which came out of the PCF shops December 15, 1948. The car was found in Columbus, Ohio in October 1969.

(Dick Argo)

Above • Seen here in the company of BREX 76057 and NP 91455 on April 25, 1970 in Othello, Washington is WFEX 68112, part of series 68000 through 68399. The 68000 series was built in May and June 1948 by American Car and Foundry Company. *(Wade Stevenson)*

Right • WFEX 68401 was one of 250 cars numbered 68400 through 68649 built in 1949 by Pacific Car and Foundry. Photo taken in January 1963. *(Paul C. Winters)*

Below • Rolling through Huntsville, Alabama In July 1969, WFEX 68854 is in a moving train with another WFEX reefer with the newer, larger GN goat monogram. Series 68650 through 69099 which includes WFEX 68854 was built in 1950 by Pacific Car and Foundry.
(Bernie Wooller)

Above • In August 1961 we see WFEX 68995 (RS), series 68650 through 69099, which was built in 1950 by Pacific Car and Foundry with Youngstown sliding flush doors. *(Paul C. Winters)*

Below •Notice that all the lettering on WFEX 76305, seen here in Huntsville, Alabama in December 1971, has been moved to the left half of the side so as to accommodate the large BN logo and Western Fruit Express inscription. The car was originally built for Burlington Refrigerator express and carried the same number but, after the merger of the Great Northern, Northern Pacific and Chicago, Burlington and Quincy the cars in this series were relettered for WFEX. This car is equipped for stage icing and has electric air circulating fans. *(Bernie Wooller)*

Right • This car has obviously been repainted since the 1972 merger of the NP, GN and CB&Q that created the BN. WHIX 70609, part of series 70290 through 70999, was built in December 1954 by Pacific Car and Foundry. The "HI" in WHIX indicates heavy insulation. *(Paul C. Winters)*

Above • WFEX 2220 was built in December 1952 by Pacific Car and Foundry. This photo was taken in December 1969. The cars were renumbered to this series after the BN merger. *(Bernie Wooler)*

Below • Western Fruit Express also operated a group of reefers with overhead bunkers in series 501 through 550. One difference between WOBX 530 shown in Columbus in October 1968 and the Fruit Growers Express reefers with overhead ice bunkers is that the FGEX cars have wood sides while this car has steel sides. *(Paul C. Winters)*

National Car Company *was a subsidiary of Fruit Growers Express. National Car, for the most part, provided refrigerator cars to the meat packing industry.*

Right • MNX 2303 was built for National Car Company in August 1955 at the CB&Q's Havelock shops in Nebraska as part of series 1800 through 2499. Some cars in this series built by FGEX, others by the CB&Q. With an AAR mechanical designation of RSM these cars were equipped with meat rails. May 20, 1964, Saddle Brook, New Jersey.
(George Berisso)

Below • The E. Kahn's Sons Company leased reefers from National Car Company from the first days of National Car's existence. EKSX 3778 and 3709 were photographed in March 1964. Both cars were part of series 3701 through 3798, were equipped with meat rails, and have been rebuilt at least once. *(Paul C. Winters)*

Right • Sioux City Dressed Beef leased cars from National Car as evidenced by NX 3039, part of series 3000 through 3049. The legend inside the black outline says, " When Empty Return to Sioux City, Iowa via Service Route." NX 3045 to the right has the same legend. These cars are in Columbus, Ohio in May 1964.
(Paul C. Winters)

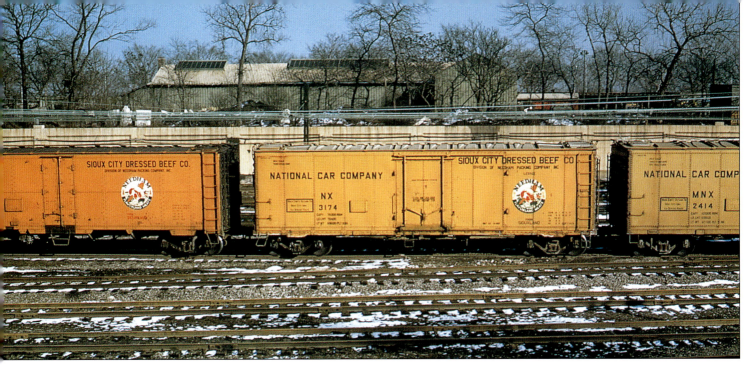

Above • These cars leased to Sioux City Dressed Beef, seen here in Chicago, Illinois in February 1968, are steel sheathed instead of wood sheathed. NX 3174 was built in May 1950. Notice that the roof is painted silver. These cars are equipped with meat rails. *(Rail Data Services collection)*

Below • MNX 2430, from series 1800 through 2499, was leased to National Packing in Kansas City. This car was built in August 1955 by the Burlington's Havelock shops and was photographed in Burlington, Iowa in January 1971. The legend in the black outline reads "When Empty Return To CB&Q Railroad Pacific Junction, Iowa Via Service Route." *(Jerry Hesley)*

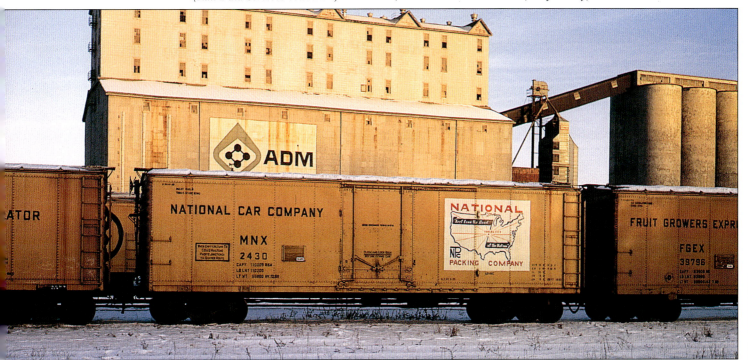

Right • Pepper Packing Company in Denver, Colorado also leased reefers from National Car's series 1800 through 2499. MNX 2330 was built in August 1955 at the Havelock shops of the CB&Q and was photographed at Pacific Junction, Iowa April 26, 1970. "When Empty Return To CB&Q Railroad Denver, Colorado Via Service Route" according to the instructions in the white outline near the reporting marks. *(Lou Schmitz)*

GENERAL AMERICAN TRANSPORTATION CORPORATION
Chicago, Illinois

General American (GATX) had its beginning in 1898 as the Atlantic Seaboard Despatch with 28 used refrigerator cars which were leased to others. Incorporated in 1902 as the German-American Car Company, the name was changed to General American about the time of World War One when feelings against anything German ran high.

In General American's early years tank cars came to be more important than refrigerator cars but all that changed when GATX began acquiring the refrigerator (and tank car) lines of other companies. Quaker City (including 2417 tank cars, 2158 refrigerator cars and 1721 stock cars) was acquired in 1928. In 1929 when General American acquired Union Refrigerator Transit (URT). Swift and Company's line was acquired in 1930 and leased back to Swift, and the Rock Island railroad's refrigerator car fleet was added in 1932. General American also leased smaller fleets to such companies as Kingan and Hygrade in the meat packing business and Libby in vegetable packing.

Most refrigerator cars owned by General American were operated and maintained by General American without regard to the reporting marks on the car. Exceptions were the cars leased to Swift and the Union Refrigerator Transit cars. Swift cars were handled separately from all other General American cars and URT continued to operate as a separate subsidiary. Swift and Union Refrigerator Transit will be dealt with in separate sections.

General American experienced a downturn in tank car construction about 1922 and sought opportunities to build other freight car types to utilize otherwise idle capacity. Among these other types, refrigerator cars soon played a large role as GATC built cars for its own lease fleet and for other customers.

Above • GARX 4505, leased to the Elgin, Joliet & Eastern, was built in December 1930 by General American as part of series 3800 through 4999. General American did not use the GARX reporting marks until the mid-1930s and at first only for refrigerator cars equipped to operate in passenger trains. The number series 3800-4999 was not listed in the *Official Railway Equipment Register* until some time around 1942, perhaps a bit earlier. Tampa, Florida. *(K. B. King, Jr., Lloyd Keyser collection)*

Below • In September 1955, GARX 940[0] leased to United Packers, rolls throug[h] Lawrence, Kansas. This car was part o[f] series 9325 through 9599.

(Don Ball collectio[n])

Top • This 1955 photo shows that KGNX 3045, from series 2900 through 3599, is a steel car except that wood has been used for the exterior because of its insulating properties.
(K. B. King, Jr., Lloyd Keyser collection)

Center • A pair of steel reefers, KGNX 3547 (left) and KGNX 3569 are in Council Bluffs, Iowa on May 29, 1954. These cars are ice-bunker refrigerator cars with meat rails. *(Lou Schmitz)*

Bottom • Apparently some boards have been replaced in the side of KGNX 3894 which carries lettering for Hygrade Food Products in August 1956 in Lawrence, Kansas.
(Don Ball collection)

Libby, McNeill & Libby operated its own modest fleet of slightly more than 100 refrigerator and pickle tank cars until the mid-1920s when the older reefers disappeared and the remaining reefers began being operated by the Quaker City Refrigerator Line. In 1928 GATC acquired Quaker City and began operating the remaining 30 or so Libby reefers. New reefers appeared soon thereafter. By 1966 Libby reefers could no longer be found in the *Official Railway Equipment Register*.

Above • The number series 1587 through 1699 did not appear until the early 1950s. LMLX 1626 was built in December 1930 and rebuilt in November 1955. Apparently this car, seen here in January 1963 at Fort Worth, Texas, was renumbered sometime during its life.
(K. B. King, Jr., Lloyd Keyser collection)

Below • LMLX 1647 was also built in December 1930 and photographed in Tampa, Florida in March 1958. This car was rebuilt in November 1955. Compare the location and orientation of the "Libby's" logo on this car and LMLX 1626. The white notice on the left half of the side under the second Libby reads "GLASS FOOD, USE CARE." *(K. B. King, Jr., Lloyd Keyser collection)*

Right • The script "Libby's" logo is absent on LMLX 1618. Instead the words "General American Transportation Corp., Owner, Libby, McNeill & Libby, Lessee" appear on the right half of the side. Near the lower left of the car side in the white field is the notice "CANNED FOOD, USE CARE." This car was built in 1930 and rebuilding was completed in November 1955. Tampa, Florida.
(K. B. King, Jr., Lloyd Keyser collection)

MERCHANTS DESPATCH TRANSPORTATION CORPORATION
Chicago, Illinois

Merchants Despatch Transportation Corporation (MDT), controlled by the New York Central, was mainly involved in the transportation of fruit and vegetables. MDT can be traced back to the last decade of the Nineteenth Century. MDT was listed as a private car owner in the 1897 *Official Railway Equipment Register*s (ORER) but in the 1920s the MDT cars were listed under the New York Central Railroad's listing in the ORER. By 1924 MDT was again listed as a private car owner with headquarters in New York, New York. By 1926 the MDT headquarters was in Rochester, New York until about 1940 when moved to Chicago, Illinois.

According to the 1930 *Moody's Manual* MDT owned or leased a total of 13,684 cars including about 8,000 cars leased from the NYC; 3,000 cars leased from the Michigan Central; and 1,300 leased from the Big Four (Cleveland, Columbus, Cincinnati & St. Louis). MDT had contracts with other lines including the Bangor & Aroostook; Maine Central; Buffalo, Rochester & Pittsburgh; Reading; Central of New Jersey; Lehigh Valley; Western Maryland and St. Louis San Francisco for the furnishing of refrigerator cars for fruit and vegetable traffic.

MDT built a large shop at East Rochester, New York which became the largest on the NYC system and produced not only refrigerator cars but also other freight cars for the NYC. In January 1929 MDT gained control of Northern Refrigerator Car Line (NRC) through ownership of the entire common stock. NRC reefers were mostly outfitted for the transportation of meat. Northern Refrigerator operated separately until it was merged into MDT about 1962.

MDT managed to survive Penn Central and Conrail albeit operating in a much reduced scope. MDT reefers could be seen all around the country. In this section you will see MDT cars in New York, Pennsylvania, Maryland, Indiana, Wisconsin, Alabama, Texas and Ontario, Canada.

APPX reporting marks (Agar Packing Company) were in use by MDT before 1950. MERX reporting marks were for the MDT controlled Mercantile Refrigerator Line. MDT did not begin using the MERX, MIDX and SUCX reporting marks until some time around 1960. NRC marks were for Northern Refrigerator cars. QMRX reporting marks came into use by MDT in the early 1950s. SUCX (Sioux City Dressed Beef Company) first appeared in the late 1950s or early 1960s. In 1988 MDT was down to four cars, all with NRBX reporting marks.

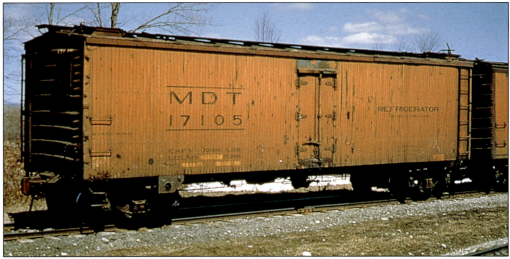

Right • MDT built most of their refrigerator cars at their own Despatch shops in East Rochester, New York. MDT 12305, part of series 11000 through 13999, was no exception. This overhead view was made in June 1974.
(George Berisso)

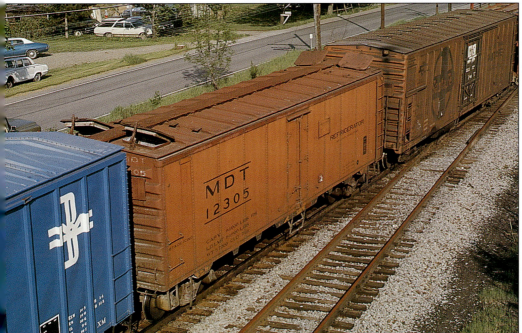

Left • MDT 17105, seen here on April 24, 1965, is part of a series of cars that first appeared about 1930. The original number series ranged from 16000 through 18999 but, in 1943, was changed to 17000 through 18999. Dimension changes in successive *Official Railway Equipment Registers* between 1931 and 1963 suggest that this series may have gone through rebuilding twice. The last rebuilding appears to have occurred about 1953 so this picture shows the final appearance of this series. The final rebuilding included altering the ice bunkers for half stage icing and equipping the cars with Preco Electric Model AA-28 air circulating fans. The "bracket" below the side sill directly under the numerals "17" is the external evidence of an air circulating fan.
(The Houser collection)

Right • MDT series 9000 through 9499, which includes MDT 9244 seen here in May 1964 in a string of reefers under catenary, were built by the Despatch Shops, Inc. in 1947. This entire series was equipped for half stage icing and had Preco FG-43 floor fans.
(The Houser collection)

Below • MDT 10376 received a new light weight in September 1954. The cars paint appears to be in good condition, perhaps repainted at the time of reweighing. MDT series 9500 through 10999 were built in 1949 or early 1950, were equipped for stage icing and had air circulating fans of the Preco FK-3 type. This photo dates from 1955.
(K. B. King, Jr. photo, Lloyd Keyser collection)

Right • MDT 11945 (RS) was part of series 11000 through 13999. These cars were equipped for stage icing and had air circulating fans. See the bracket below the KarTrak label. MDT 11945 was in Conway, Pennsylvania on November 24, 1984.
(Gordon Lloyd, Jr., Matthew J. Herson, Jr. collection)

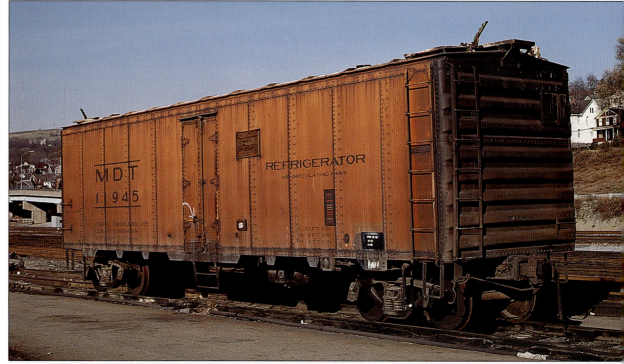

Right • MDT 11957 is being rerailed by two wreckers at Laflin, Pennsylvania on March 3, 1963.
(Edward S. Miller)

Below • Among the details seen here on MDT 12523 in Selkirk, New York May 1, 1977 is the Miner D-3290 XL hand brake. Series 11000 through 13999 were equipped for stage icing and many different kinds of air circulating fans. Cars 12200 to 12699 had Equipco model M-289-3 overhead fans.
(Matthew J. Herson, Jr. collection)

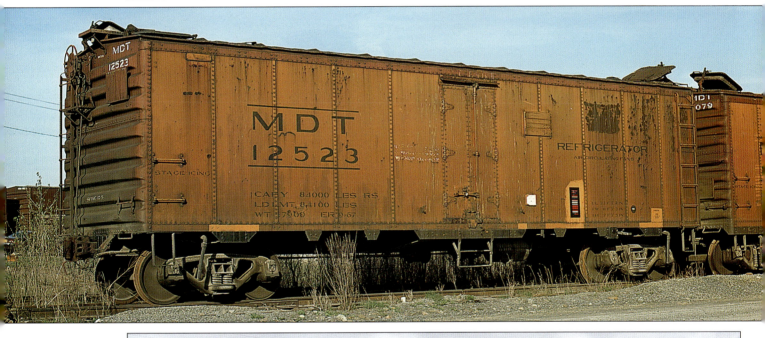

Right • MDT 12555 (RS) from series 11000 through 13999 was photographed in Huntsville, Alabama in May 1972. Some cars from this series bore the logo of the New York Central. Others did not. No pattern emerged from an examination of the slides available for this book.
(Bernie Wooller)

Above • A very dirty MDT 13093, from series 11000 through 13999, is at 59th Street yard in Milwaukee, Wisconsin on August 25, 1979. *(Ronald A Plazzotta)*

Right • This shot of the B end of MDT 13405, taken February 26, 1983 in Indianapolis, Indiana, affords an opportunity to study some of the end details such as the Miner D-3290-XL hand brake and the Standard Improved Dreadnaught ends. Modelers use the notation R2/4 to describe this Dreadnaught end which has one large rectangular rib and two regular ribs in the top section and four ribs in the bottom section. *(James Mischke)*

Above • One can almost feel and hear the rush as this string of cars, including MDT 13505 bearing an Illinois Central logo, speeds past the photographer in electrified New Haven Railroad territory in January 1973. A couple of BAR reefers are to the right of MDT 13505.

(Don Ball collection)

Above • It looks like MDT 13563 was "cornered" recently. This shot was taken in Windsor, Ontario in November 1977. As can be seen in this and some of the preceding photos, some MDT reefers bore the emblem of a railroad, some bore none. *(Lloyd Keyser collection)*

Below • Here's another example of an MDT reefer, in this case number 13593, bearing an Illinois Central logo on the right half of the side. It is July 1972. *(George Berisso)*

Right • This is both a good angle and good light conditions to see some of the details such as the drain hose hanging down beside the nearest truck or the Miner D-3290-XL hand brake on MDT 13636 as it stands in Garland, Texas in May 1971. *(Lloyd Keyser collection)*

Above • Apparently the light weight, capacity and load limit have been restenciled at some point. MDT 13715 could use a cleaning as it stands in Baltimore, Maryland in December 1988. *(Jim Rogers)*

Below • MDT 13821 (RS), series 11000 through 13999, was photographed at 59th Street in Milwaukee, Wisconsin on August 25, 1979. If there was a pattern as to whether or not cars from series 11000 through 13999 bore the herald of some railroad, it is not very apparent. *(Ronald A Plazzotta)*

Above • Series 14000 through 14199 had plug instead of hinged doors. MDT 14025 is in Syracuse, New York on May 23, 1978. *(Randy Garnhart)*

Below • MDT 14079, in Selkirk, New York on May 1, 1977, is equipped for stage icing and has air circulating fans. Someone cleaned off the ACI label on the right half of the side. The KarTrak scanners had difficulty reading dirty labels so eventually use of the KarTrak system was abandoned.
(Matthew J. Herson, Jr. collection)

Right • APPX reporting marks first appeared some time between 1948 and 1950 on cars leased from MDT by the Agar Packing Company. APPX 319, an all-steel reefer in APPX series 300 through 399, is in Columbus, Ohio on April 26, 1963.
(Paul C. Winters)

Above • APPX 401 is being switched at Detroit Harbor Terminal, Detroit, Michigan, in July 1959. The wood-sided car appears to be freshly painted and if the reweigh date is any indication, it was repainted in June 1959. This car would have been built in 1936 or 1937. Wood sides were used because of the presumed insulating qualities wood possessed. The square-corner Dreadnaught ends were not produced after about 1940 and the production run of what appears to be a Universal 2050 hand brake was a brief period around 1940. *(Emery J. Gulash, Morning Sun Books collection)*

Below • MERX reporting marks were for the MDT-controlled Mercantile Refrigerator Line which first appeared in the mid-1930s. MERX 434, standing in Binghamton, New York in July 1972, is an ice-bunker reefer with meat rails from series 430 through 599 leased to National Packing. *(Dick Argo)*

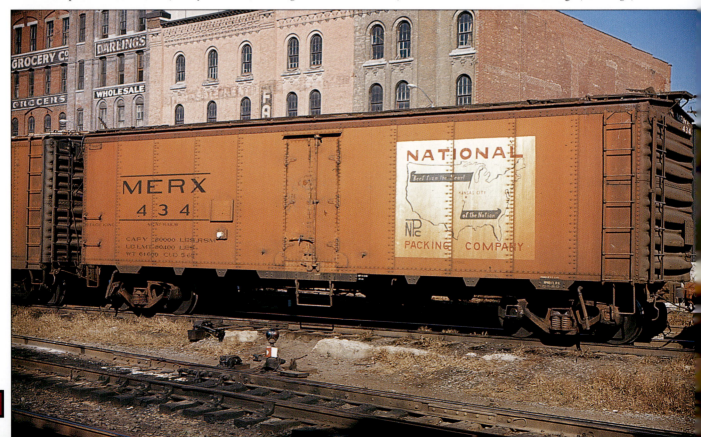

Above • MERX 547 was in Council Bluffs, Iowa on February 12, 1967. Notice the drain hoses that hang down over the trucks.
(Lou Schmitz)

Right • This close-up of the National Packing Company emblem shows that the dimensional data and date built usually found on the right half a the car side are completely missing. This is the side of MERX 547 (above).
(Lou Schmitz)

Below • MERX 902 is leased to Oscar Mayer obviously enough. It is November 27, 1955 here in Council Bluffs, Iowa. In the early 1930s Oscar Mayer's refrigerator cars came from Standard Refrigerator Car Company and General American Tank Car Company but eventually switched to MDT. This car was built before 1937. *(Lou Schmitz)*

Right • Both MERX 908 seen here in Lawrence, Kansas in August 1956 and MERX 902 in the previous picture have wood sides but are otherwise all-steel cars.
(Don Ball collection)

Above • MIDX 122 was in Huntsville, Alabama in March 1971, a long way from its Luverne, Minnesota home of Minnesota Iowa and Dakotas Packing Company. This car is equipped with meat rails and half stage icing. *(Bernie Wooller)*

Below • Iowa Beef Packers, Incorporated is sometimes credited with being the firm that changed the meat packing industry. Traditionally meat was processed by highly skilled and highly paid butchers who made all the cuts in a side of beef or pork. IBP used low skilled, nonunion meat cutters who made the same cut on each slab of meat as it came by on an assembly line sort of process. IBPX 700, leased from MDT, is seen here in May 1975 and is equipped with meat rails.
(David Nelson photo, David H. Hickcox collection)

Above • QMRX 52131 is an older car than others we have seen in this section. Both sides and ends are wood and the hand brake is the vertical staff type not applied to cars after 1937. This shot was taken sometime after May 1954.
(Emery J. Gulash, Morning Sun Books collection)

Below • SUCX 118 is in Tampa, Florida in 1957. The car has steel ends and wood sides. This series of cars would have been built about 1936 or 1937. *(K. B. King, Jr. photo, Lloyd Keyser collection)*

Left • Steel ends are visible in this undated shot of SUCX 134 at an unknown location.
(Morning Sun Books collection)

Above • Dairy Shippers Despatch Company used refrigerator cars from three sources. DSDX owned some of the cars they used and leased others from National Car Company. Series 200-799, however, was leased from Merchants Despatch. It must be a cold day in April 1960 in Goldsboro, North Carolina as evidenced by the icicles on DSDX 437. *(K.B. King, Jr., Lloyd Keyser collection)*

Below • NRC 16009 (RS) bears the logo of the Illinois Central in this photo taken in August 1971 at Neosho, Missouri.
(Lloyd Keyser collection)

Top • NRC 16260 (RS) was in Dallas, Texas in February 1964. The shadow along the edge of the roof reveals the overhanging lip typical of roofs applied by the Despatch shops. *(Lloyd Keyser collection)*

Center • NRC 16444 (RS), series 16000 through 16799, was photographed in June 1973. Usually fresh patches of paint indicate some change or removal of stenciling on the car side but the clean area at the lower left of this car's side is the result of a repair. The small letters under the word REFRIGERATOR on the right side reads "air circulating fans." *(Paul C. Winters)*

Bottom • NRC 16502, sporting a more modern Illinois Central herald was photographed on March 31, 1974 in Omaha, Nebraska. *(Gordon E. Lloyd)*

Above • NRC 16753 (RS) has had the paint touched up here and there. The lower left yellow is immediately above the freshly painted black bracket for the pulley to power the air circulating fan when the car is stationary. The date is May 2, 1975, the place is Schiller Park, Illinois *(Raymond F. Kucaba)*

Below • Unlike the other all-steel reefers seen in this section, NRC 19040 (RS) has flat steel ends. This car was in Huntsville, Alabama in March 1970 for this photo. *(Bernie Wooller)*

Below • The round plate around the air circulating fan shaft is readily visible in this January 1968 photo of NRC 19190 (RS), series 18500 through 19299. *(Rail Data Services collection)*

64

Above • Fresh paint adorns NRC 19414 (RS), series 19400 through 19499, in November 1962 at the yards at Joyce Avenue in Columbus, Ohio. *(Paul C. Winters)*

Below • The Gulf, Mobile and Ohio herald gradually disappeared from cars after the merger with the Illinois Central. Fortunately for us we get to see one on NRC 19745 (RS), series 19500 through 19749, on August 25, 1979, at 59th St., Milwaukee, Wisconsin. *(Raymond F. Kucaba)*

MORRELL, RATH AND THE MATHER STOCK CAR COMPANY
Chicago, Illinois

In 1881 Alonzo Clark Mather (1848-1941) developed a stock car which won an award from the American Humane Society in 1883. Eventually the Mather Horse and Stock Car Company's equipment included box, stock and refrigerator cars of Mather's own design. These cars were characterized by the use of common lumber and structural steel shapes readily available to all industries. This use of ordinary materials meant that Mather cars were cheap and easy to repair almost anywhere. An exception to the use of common materials was the roof which was of Mather's own unique design. All in all the Mather designed cars presented a distinctive appearance that was readily recognizable.

It was between 1932 and 1937 that the Mather (now named Mather Stock Car Company) refrigerator car fleet grew from 225 reefers to 930 ice bunker refrigerator cars. By 1943 the Mather fleet had more than doubled to 2428 and about half (1308) were refrigerator cars. Virtually the entire Mather reefer fleet was outfitted to haul packing house products as the cars had either brine tanks or meat rails.

Mather leased refrigerator cars to, among other companies, Agar Packing & Provision Co. (AGRX), Hygrade Food Products Corp. (HFPX), Hunter Packing Co. (HPAX), Kohrs Packing Company (KOHX), John Morrell & Co. (MORX), Peyton Packing Co. (PPCX), Rath Packing Co. (RPRX), as well as, on a short-term basis, leasing cars with Mather's own reporting marks of MRRX or MUNX. Mather was acquired by North American Car Corporation in the summer of 1955. This section will include a few cars built under North American after Mather ceased to exist but which carried reporting marks originally used by Mather or one of Mather's lessees.

Above • MORX 9021 (RSM), part of series 9000 through 9199, originally built and owned by Mather, has an old Klasing hand brake which was typical of Mather reefers, Photo made on 1955 at Tampa, Florida.
(K.B. King, Jr., Lloyd Keyser collection)

Below • Morrell continued to operate their own refrigerator car line until late 1954 when the cars were sold to Mather. MRX 5649 (RSM) is from this last series of 500 reefers, 5500 through 5699. These cars were built for Morrell in 1939 by General American. Ten cars, although not this one, from this series were built using specially manufactured plywood instead of matched lumber. By the time this photo was made in May 1958 at Chicago, Illinois this car had passed from Morrell ownership to Mather and finally, in the summer of 1955, to North American Car Company. *(Emery J. Gulash, Morning Sun Books collection)*

Left • MORX 9293 (RSM), built in March 1940 by Mather was part of series 9200 through 9974 Photo made on July 4, 1971 at Ashland, Wisconsin.
(Owen Leander)

Below • MORX 9465 (RSM) was built by Mather. Photo made on July 26, 1969 at Ashland, Wisconsin. Cars in series 9200 through 9974 would have been equipped with wood running boards when built. *(Owen Leander)*

Left • Low angle lighting allows us to see the bottom edge of the steel truss that supported the sides of Mather cars whether box, stock or reefer. It is something of an oversimplification to say that Mather added insulation and exterior sheathing to their box cars to create refrigerator cars. MORX 9900 (RSM) on the right and MORX 9898 were both part of series 9200 through 9974 and are fairly representative of wood side refrigerator car construction in the early 1940s. Mather built both cars.
(Morning Sun Books collection)

Above • It appears that MORX 9904 (RSM) has received the benefit of a rather recent coat of paint. The date and location of this photo are unknown.
(Morning Sun Books collection)

Below • Rath Packing Company was headquartered in Waterloo, Iowa and, into the early 1930s leased refrigerator cars from General American but by 1937 Rath was leasing from Mather. RPRX 358 (RSM) from series 100 through 599 was built in December 1948 by Mather. This view was taken in Council Bluffs, Iowa September 11, 1965. *(Lou Schmitz)*

Left • RPRX 547 RSM, series 100 through 599, was built in August 1952 by Mather. Details of the Dreadnaught ends and Universal hand brake are visible in this shot taken July 4, 1971 in Ashland, Wisconsin.
(Owen Leander)

Above • Rath Packing Company's RPRX 562 (RSM) is stenciled as being built in September 1952 by Mather and photographed in Ashland, Wisconsin on July 4, 1971. It is not clear whether this car was new in 1952 or rebuilt in 1952. *(Owen Leander)*

Below • Another Rath reefer, this time RPRX 600 (RSM) from series 600 through 999, is photographed in Ashland, Wisconsin on July 4, 1971. This car was built in December 1952 by Mather. *(Owen Leander)*

Above • Mather built this reefer in December of 1952. RPRX 605 (RSM) is part of series 600 through 999 and is in Tampa, Florida in 1957 in this view. This car has a small version of the Rath logo. *(K. B. King, Jr., Lloyd Keyser collection)*

Below • A larger version of the Rath logo enclosed in a rectangle adorns RPRX 612 (RSM) from series 600 through 999. This Mather built car was photographed July 4, 1971 in Ashland, Wisconsin. *(Owen Leander)*

Right • RPRX 629 (RSM) is in Ashland, Wisconsin July 4, 1971. This car, also part of series 600 through 999 was built in September 1953 by Mather. Given the late date of this photo and the quantitiy of older, wood-sheathed reefers, these cars may be at the end of their useful life and awaiting scrapping or other disposition. *(Owen Leander)*

Right • Compare the color of the end on RPRX 635 (RSM) seen here July 4, 1971 in Ashland, Wisconsin and RPRX 629 in the previous photo. Were the ends of some of these reefers painted a different color or are we seeing the results of weather? This car was built in December 1953.
(Owen Leander)

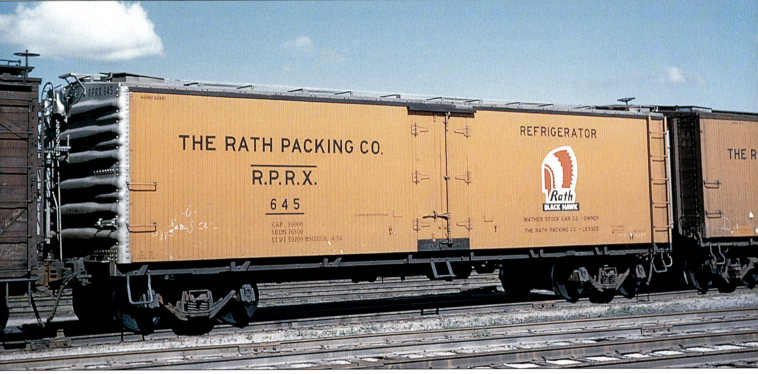

Above • It is very clear that the ends and roof of RPRX 645 (RSM) have been painted a different color than the sides. The date is May 29, 1954, the place Council Bluffs, Iowa. *(Lou Schmitz)*

Below • Two features clearly visible in this photo of RPRX 802 (RSM) from series 600 through 999 are wood ends with added reinforcements and the unusual early Klasing geared hand brake. This car dates from March 1923 but the Klasing hand brake was not produced until years later so we may be looking at a rebuilt car which is seen here in Waterloo, Iowa in 1958. *(W. L. Heitter)*

Above • This repair facility (RIP track or Repair-In-Place track) is located in Waterloo, Iowa and is apparently dedicated to the maintenance of reefers leased to Rath. RPRX 835 (RSM), series 600 through 999, was built by Mather in March 1923 and probably has been rebuilt as evidenced by the reinforcement of the wood ends and the early and unusual Klasing geared hand brake. This photo was taken in 1958. *(W. L. Heitter)*

Left • This photo was taken in San Antonio, Texas in January 1969. With North American's acquisition of the Mather Stock Car Company, the construction of cars to Mather's designs ceased. RPRX 688 (RSM) is a more modern all-steel car. *(Ed Stoll, Lloyd Keyser collection)*

Below • This more modern, plug-door refrigerator car, RPRX 1533 (RSM), series 1505 through 1554, is leased to Rath from North American Car Corporation which acquired Mather and the RPRX reporting marks in 195. The car was built only a few years before this May 1960 photo.
(Jim Konas, Randy Garnhart collection)

Right • This shot dates from April 1972 but the location was not recorded. Rath's RPRX 1632 (RSM) sports a plug-door, Universal hand brake and Dreadnaught ends. Compare the large but simple Rath logo in the rectangle on this car with the smaller logo on the preceding car.
(David Nelson, David H. Hickcox collection)

Below • By joining two refrigerator cars semi-permanently the shipper received a more advantageous rate. Here we see RPRX 701A and 701B (RSM) on September 5, 1971 at Council Bluffs, Iowa. These cars have apparently had hinged doors replaced with larger sliding plug doors.
(Lou Schmitz)

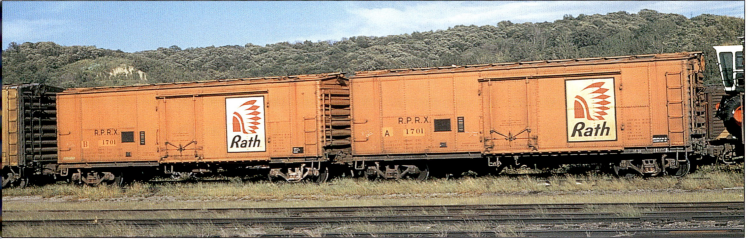

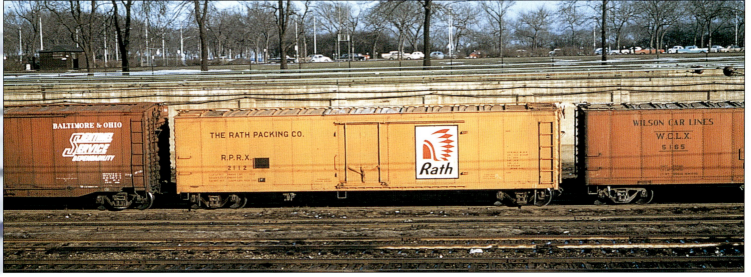

Above • Meat reefers of this length are far less common than cars of forty foot inside length or less. RPRX 2112 (RSM), built February 1961 and part of series 2101 through 2114, had an inside length of 43 feet and five inches. This photo dates from February 1968 in Chicago, Illinois. *(Rail Data Services collection)*

Below • RPRX series 2115 through 2199, which includes RPRX 2115 (RSM) seen here at Council Bluffs, Iowa August 1, 1971, had a total length of over 55 feet and an inside length of 46'-10". *(Lou Schmitz)*

NORTH AMERICAN CAR CORPORATION
Chicago, Illinois

North American Car Corporation had its beginnings before 1922 as a tank car leasing company. By 1931 North American was also operating refrigerator cars and one stock car. The NADX fleet had grown to more than 1700 refrigerator cars and more than 4000 tank cars. In 1955 NWX was purchased by North American Car which eventually added their own logo to the sides of some cars but retained the NWX reporting marks. NWX cars will be covered in a separate section. North American was taken over by General Electric Railcar in 1984 and continues in the car leasing business.

Above • NADX series 100 through 299, which included NADX 159 (RSM) seen here in Chicago, Illinois in May 1958, was built by Pacific Car and Foundry in September 1954. *(Emery J. Gulash, Morning Sun Books collection)*

Below • NADX 215 (RSM), another car from NADX series 100 through 299, also built in September 1954 by Pacific Car and Foundry, bears a different lettering arrangement than NADX 159 seen previously. Photo made on July 4, 1971 at Ashland, Wisconsin. *(Owen Leander)*

Above • Lehigh & Hudson River Alco locomotives 3 and 10 are about to pass NADX 297 (RSM) on June 4, 1960 at Maybrook, New York. Mostly hidden behind the locomotives is a Swift reefer while coupled to the other end of NADX 297 is a reefer leased to the Rath Packing Company of Waterloo, Iowa. In the distance is a green and yellow reefer from NWX. *(Edward S. Miller)*

Below • It is June 13, 1964 in Croxton, New Jersey and we see NADX 423 (RS), series 400 through 499, which has wood sides and Improved Dreadnaught ends. *(Richard Zmijewski)*

Above • A much newer NADX 965 (RSM) from series 900 through 999 is seen standing at Council Bluffs, Iowa on May 11, 1968. This car was rebuilt in May 1957 but must have recently been repainted. The Hormel logo is unusual if not unique. *(Lou Schmitz)*

Above and Right • NADX 3874 (RSM) was in Council Bluffs, Iowa on April 15, 1961. Our photographer photographed the entire car and took a close-up of the Greenlee Packing Company emblem. It can clearly be seen that this car, part of series 3800 through 3864 was built in March of 1961. *(Lou Schmitz)*

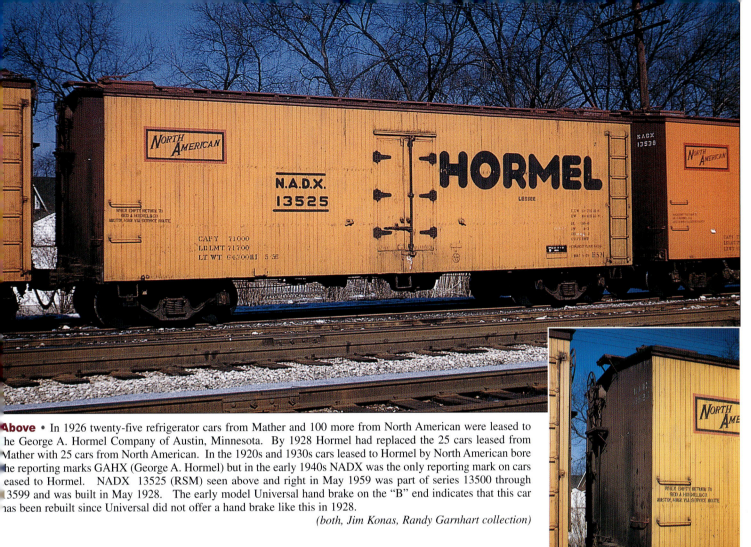

Above • In 1926 twenty-five refrigerator cars from Mather and 100 more from North American were leased to the George A. Hormel Company of Austin, Minnesota. By 1928 Hormel had replaced the 25 cars leased from Mather with 25 cars from North American. In the 1920s and 1930s cars leased to Hormel by North American bore the reporting marks GAHX (George A. Hormel) but in the early 1940s NADX was the only reporting mark on cars leased to Hormel. NADX 13525 (RSM) seen above and right in May 1959 was part of series 13500 through 13599 and was built in May 1928. The early model Universal hand brake on the "B" end indicates that this car has been rebuilt since Universal did not offer a hand brake like this in 1928.

(both, Jim Konas, Randy Garnhart collection)

Below • Albert Lea, Minnesota, the location of this shot taken in September 1968, was home to a Wilson and Company meat packing plant. This car, a former Mather car was originally lettered for Morrell as can be seen by the shape of the clean paint areas but has been renumbered NADX 4569. The Hormel lettering probably resembled the car above. The Hormel car behind NADX 4569 is NACX 188. North American Car Company acquired Mather in the summer of 1955. *(Jerry Hesley)*

NORTH WESTERN REFRIGERATOR LINE COMPANY
Chicago, Illinois

North Western Refrigerator Line Company (NWRL) was known for two distinctions. The color schemes used were something other than the more typical yellow or orange and the NWRL shops were the former winter quarters of the Ringling Brothers Circus in Baraboo, Wisconsin. The Baraboo shops had been empty since 1918 when Ringling merged with Barnum and Bailey. These same facilities have been home to the Circus World Museum since 1959.

North Western Refrigerator Line always had a close relationship with the Chicago and North Western Railway Company (C&NW) but was not owned by the C&NW. The C&NW gave preferential treatment to NWX cars and NWX provided the C&NW with added revenues in the form of additional traffic. The NWRL fleet was about tenth in size when compared to the fleets of other private-owner refrigerator car lines.

NWRL began with second hand thirty six foot, wood underframe reefers. July 1926 saw the first order for new refrigerator cars from American Car & Foundry. Unlike the second hand cars this first new car order was for refrigerator cars of forty foot length. NWRL cars were painted gray with boxcar red ends and roof until very early 1953 when NWRL began to replace the gray sides with the well-known yellow and green. During the 1930s many NWRL reefers bore the colorful "billboard" advertising for quite a number of Midwest producers of eggs, poultry, milk, cheese, produce and so on. All bore a logo similar to that of the C&NW logo to show their close association with that railroad. All these colorful paint schemes were gone by 1937 or shortly thereafter.

North Western Refrigerator Line conducted three major rebuilding programs in 1952 (124 cars), 1953 (276 cars) and 1955 (224 cars). The first was conducted in shops in Wisconsin while the second and third programs were done by Pacific Car & Foundry in Renton, Washington.

North American Car Company bought NWRL in 1955 but the close relationship with the C&NW continued after 1955. The NWRL fleet remained intact and separate until about 1964 when some Mather cars were renumbered, given NWX reporting marks and repainted in the classic NWRL yellow and green. North American closed the NWRL's Baraboo shops in December 1963 as new mechanical refrigerator cars were being purchased and car rebuilding was no longer needed. By 1978, only 25 NWX cars were left in service. Six years later, North American was taken over by General Electric Railcar. What few cars remained were stored and soon dismantled.

Below • Silhouetted against the sky, NWX 12001 (RS) presents the classic NWRL reefer image so fondly remembered by so many people. The earliest know application of the green and yellow paint was in very early 1953 at the Baraboo shops. The reefers in series 12000 through 12300 were built in April and May 1931 and were rebuilt by Pacific Car & Foundry in Renton, Washington beginning in 1953. This particular car was rebuilt in July 1953 when it would have had this green and yellow paint applied instead of the earlier gray. This rebuilding gave the car a steel roof and ends, a power Equipco hand brake and exposed side sills. NWX 12001 is fresh from rebuilding when this photo was taken in Bozeman, Montana on August 10, 1953.
(Wade Stevenson)

Left • The earlier gray of North Western Refrigerator Line is seen in February 1949 on NWX 1278 (RS), series 1000 through 3899. This classic old reefer has both ends and sides sheathed in wood, the hand brake is still the old AAR standard vertical shaft type and the running boards are wood. The location of this photo is not recorded.
(Carl Solheim collection)

Right • NWX 4425 (RS) has the deeper center sill of the July 1926 order (ACF lot number 122). The cars were originally numbered 6001 through 6200 and were later renumbered into the series 4000 through 5499. At the end of its useful life, as evidenced by the white line through the reporting marks, NWX 4425 (RS), built in March 1926, stands next to Highway 53 in LaCrosse, Wisconsin on June 27, 1981. Although little changed from its original appearance, except for paint, braces barely visible here have been added between side and center sills. Three different individuals submitted photos of this car at this exact spot taken in 1979, 1980 and 1981.
(Lloyd Keyser collection)

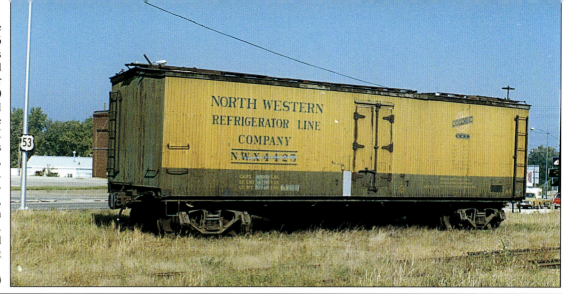

Above • Starting with the cars delivered in 1927, all or almost all of the reefers built for NWRL before NWRL was acquired by North American were built by American Car & Foundry, all to a design similar to that shown here. In April and May 1927 ACF built 1,020 reefers as their lot 404 and these cars were first numbered in NWX series 6701 through 7720. By 1937 this series was being renumbered into the 15000 through 15999 series. The date and location of this photo are unrecorded but stenciling on the side of NWX 15356 (RS) indicates that the picture was taken before 1954. *(Arthur E. Mitchell)*

Below • NWX 5019 (RS), series 4000 through 5499, was built by American Car & Foundry in April 1927. This photo was taken in Omaha, Nebraska on January 15, 1955. *(Lou Schmitz)*

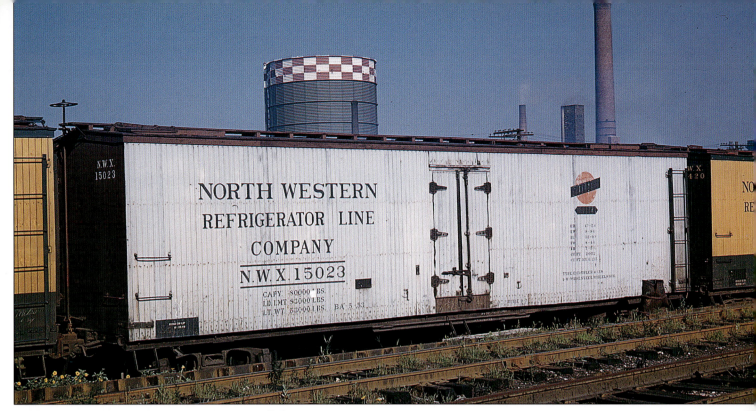

Above • As if to illustrate that cars still painted in the gray with box car red ends lasted well past the beginning of the the green and yellow we have this shot of NWX 15023 taken on August 16, 1960 at an unknown location.
(Karl C. Henkels, W. Woelfer collection)

Below • This nice photograph of NWX 70159 taken March 19, 1955 in Omaha, Nebraska allows us to point out a feature of herald or logo on the right half of the car side. The stenciling is composed of only two colors, red and black. The yellow letters are merely the color of the car side showing through where no other paint was applied. While this herald is similar to that of the Chicago & North Western Railway the words are different. The angled bar has the words NORTH WESTERN, REFRIGERATOR appears in the top of the circle, LINE across the bottom of the circle and reporting marks NWX in the bar below.
(Lou Schmitz)

Left • The 'fishbelly' underframe is nicely silouetted in this shot taken March 27, 1952 at the C&NW's Proviso Yard, Chicago, Illinois. NWX 15100 (RS) was built in May 1927 by American Car & Foundry (ACF). There were 1020 cars, originally numbered from 7000 through 8019 which were built in April and May 1927 by ACF. These cars were renumbered from the 7000 series into series 15000 through 15999 before 1937.
*(William Fuka
Lloyd Keyser collection)*

Right • The B end (hand brake end) of NWX 3748 peeks out from behind NWX 10530 (RS) in this undated shot. NWX 10530 is one of the rebuilt cars from the NWRL's first rebuilding program in 1952. This first rebuilding program took place in the Green Bay & Western shops at Green Bay, Wisconsin, in the Chicago, St. Paul, Minneapolis & Omaha shops at Hudson, Wisconsin and in NWX's own Baraboo, Wisconsin shops. These early rebuilds received Improved Dreadnaught ends and diagonal braces at the lower corners of the sides but retained the original composite (wood) ends and vertical staff hand brake. It is most likely that this car was painted gray upon rebuilding and later repainted this green and yellow.
(Pete Dumouie, Lloyd Keyser collection)

Above • NWX 12126 (RS) which was built in April 1927 was rebuilt at Pacific Car & Foundy's Renton, Washington facility in 1953. This particular car was rebuilt in August 1953. It can be seen on these rebuilds that the end sill protrudes beyond the outer face of the steel end. This scene is in Wisconsin Rapids, Wisconsin on July 26, 1969. *(Rail Data Services collection)*

Below • NWX 12145 (RS), part of series 12000 through 12300 rebuilt by PC&F in 1953, is seen here apparently still in service in this shot taken sometime after September 1966. The first impression is that 12145 seems to have held up rather well until we remind ourselves that wood cars were repainted as often as every three years. *(M. Zak collection)*

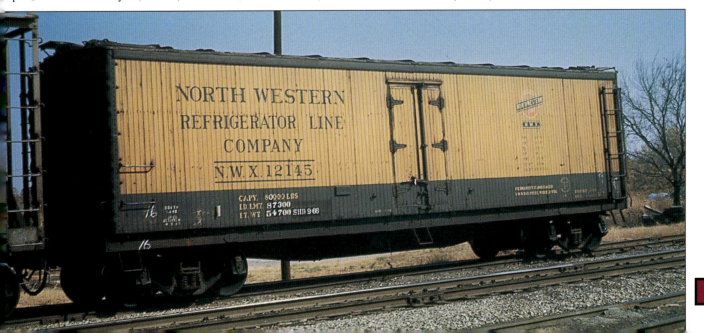

Right • Compare the appearance of NWX 12146 (RS), seen here in Othello, Washington on August 29, 1953 fresh from rebuilding by Pacific Car & Foundry, with sister car NWX 12145 in the previous photo. Rebuilding added a steel roof in place of the original wood roof. Notice that the roof is unpainted galvanized metal except that the hatches and two end panels of the roof are painted the same color as the ends. Notice further that the end of the running board protruding beyond the end of the car is painted to match the end but the rest of the running board is unpainted, galvanized metal. The 1953 rebuilding program produced 276 'Renton rebuilds' which are essentiall all steel except for the sides. *(Wade Stevenson)*

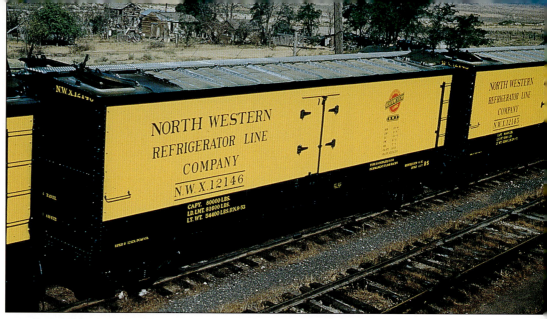

Left • This shot of NWX 1203 (RS) and NWX 791 (RS) allows comparison of the 1953 and 195 'Renton Rebuilds.' When rebuilt b Pacific Car & Foundry and renum bered into series 12000 throug 12300 the 1953 rebuilds receive Dreadnaught ends with one narro rectangular rib and three regular rib in the top half and three regular rib in the bottom section. (Modele use the notation r+3/3 for this end NWX 791, to the right, is taller afte rebuilding and has ends with on large rectangular rib and two regula ribs in the top half and four regula ribs in the bottom section (Modelers notation is R+2/4 Other features of the 1953 'Rento Rebuilds' include wood siding th now ends immediately above th side sill and, not visible here, power hand brake from Equipc Stencilling on the side of the ca indicates NWX 12038 (RS) wa built in April 1927 and rebuilt August 1953. This photo fro November 1971 was taken Clyman Junction, Chicago, Illinois *(Ronald A. Plazzott*

Below • NWX 600 (RS), series 600 through 899, is representative of the 1955 group of 224 'Renton Rebuilds.' These 224 cars were rebuilt essentially the same as the 1953 group of 276 cars except that sides are steel and the cars are taller. The differences in the ends have already been described. This car has been repainted at least once, in July 1960, since being rebuilt in 1955. This photo was taken in Omaha, Nebraska on July 9, 1961. *(Lou Schmitz)*

Above • The reinforcing braces added to many, if not most, NWRL reefers are visible in this photo of NWX 15120 (RS) taken in Lawrence, Kansas in October 1955. The braces angle downward from the side sill, pass under the center sill and then go up to the side sill on the other side. Any car receiving heavy repairs after 1960 received a set of these braces. *(Don Ball)*

Below • We must deal with one last group of 'NWX' refrigerator cars before we close this look at the North Western Refrigerator Line although, technically speaking, the car in the photo below is not a refrigerator car. Fifty cars in series 16000 through 16049 and 350 NWRL refrigerator cars in the series 16050 through 16399 appeared in 1964 and 1965. The first 50 cars had composite (wood) ends while the remaining 350 had steel ends as seen in this photo. Remember that North American acquired both Mather and North Western Refrigerator Line in the mid-1950s. Close examination of the car in this photo, NWX 16272 (RB), reveals that it is a Mather built car marked with the mechanical designation 'RB.' These former Mather cars had their ice bunkers removed, the hatches sealed, were been repainted in North Western Refrigerator Line colors and given NWX reporting marks. The car is, at this stage in its career, an insulated box car marked "BUILT 12-49" although it is not clear whether Mather was actually building or only rebuilding cars at that late date. *(Charles Yungkurth, Lloyd Keyser collection)*

PACIFIC FRUIT EXPRESS

Among the privately owned refrigerator car fleets it is probably safe to say that Pacific Fruit Express (PFE) was the largest. Two private freight car companies had more cars - General American Transportation Corporation and Union Tank Car Company - but when only reefers are considered, PFE was probably the largest with approximately 36,000 cars at the company's zenith.

PFE has its origins in the early years of the 20th century while both the Southern Pacific (SP) and the Union Pacific (UP) were under the control of E. H. Harriman. Pacific Fruit Express (PFE) was formed to provide refrigerator cars to both lines. PFE had placed its first order for 6000 refrigerator cars and was up and running by 1907. In 1908 the US Government began action to break up the UP/SP combination. PFE, being jointly owned by the UP and SP continued, however, to serve its original purpose which was to provide the refrigerator cars and the protective services of icing, ventilation and heating.

Beginning in the middle of 1923 Pacific Fruit Express cars began to appear bearing the Western Pacific's (WP) logo on the side instead of the UP and/or SP logos. More on the WP cars later.

Not only was the PFE reefer fleet relatively large but PFE reefers traveled to virtually every corner of the US. PFE had very little involvement with carrying meat and meat products but PFE was deeply involved in hauling the produce of California's fertile valleys all over the country.

Left • This shot was taken in Dallas, Texas August 1960 and shows that reefers with wo[od] sides could last a long time. The R-30-24 a[nd] R-40-24 classes were rebuilt from earlier cla[ss]es of cars and those with 30-ton underfram[es] were classes R-30-24 while those with 40-t[on] underframes were classes R-40-24. T[he] rebuilding program stripped the cars to th[e] underframe and completely new superstru[c]tures were built. Sides were plywood and en[ds] were of the "Improved Dreadnaught" ty[pe] which had little ribs between the larger ri[bs]. The plywood sides didn't work as well [as] expected and when necessary the plywood w[as] replaced with tongue and groove lumber as [on] PFE 66759 here which was built in July 19[23] and rebuilt May 1948. The paint and letteri[ng] arrangement seen here is that applied in 19[46] and later.

(Richard Kuelbs pho[to] Lloyd Keyser collectio[n])

Below • What we see here is an older car from class R-30-12, R-30-13 or R-30-14 rebuilt with a solid steel roof among other improvements and reclassified as R-30-16. PFE 76189, class R-30-16, from number series 73001 through 76554, is seen here on February 8, 1952 in Dubuque, Iowa. The cars were rebuilt and reclassified into R-30-16 before the 1946 stenciling chan[ge] that put both the SP and UP heralds on both sides of the car. The conditi[on] of the car is the result of about 10 years of accumulated grime.

(W.L. Heitte[r])

Left • The class R-30-24 cars were reefers rebuilt with Dreadnaught ends and plywood sides. PFE 66480, from R-30-24 series 65921 through 68532, was photographed in Dallas, Texas in August 1966. This paint scheme would have been applied when the car was built.
(Richard Kuelbs photo, Lloyd Keyser collection)

Right • PFE was an early user of all-steel refrigerator cars and an example of one of the first all-steel classes, R-40-10, is preserved at the Orange Empire Railway Museum, Perris, California, photographed in July 1996. PFE 43535, series 43201 through 43700, built in March 1937, is stenciled in the post-1946 arrangement, not in the as delivered scheme.
(Lloyd Keyser collection)

Above • One of the features that helps identify this car's age is the L square-corner Dreadnaught ends which can be seen here in this July 1987 photo in Perris, California, of PFE 43535. *(Lloyd Keyser collection)*

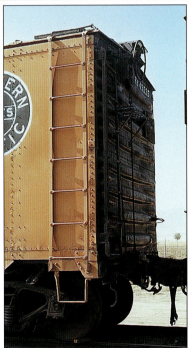

Above • This view of the end shows the unusual early Ureco Type V hand brake and Dreadnaught "4/4" ends. (the "4/4" refers to four ribs above the center seam and four ribs below.)
(Lloyd Keyser collection)

Right • PFE 5529, R-40-23, series 5001 through 6000, was built in 1947 by Mt. Vernon. This photo is from October 1970 in Huntsville, Alabama. These were the first series to be built after the 1946 stenciling change. As delivered the Southern Pacific herald would have been placed nearest the door on both sides. Later practice, as seen here, placed the Southern Pacific herald nearest the "B" or hand brake end of the car. *(Bernie Wooller)*

Below • Pacific Car and Foundry also built class R-40-23 reefers and PFE 48444, seen here in October 1968, is an example. The PC&F cars, part of series 48203 through 48702, were built in 1947. *(Paul C. Winters)*

Above • Union Pacific wrecker 03042 lifts PFE 3208, class R-40-25, series 2001 through 5000, in Council Bluffs, Iowa on August 9, 1956. *(Lou Schmitz)*

Above • PFE class R-40-25 reefers were built between 1949 and 1950 by the Southern Pacific Equipment Company and were numbered in series 2001 through 5000. PFE 4130 was photographed in Garland, Texas in March 1973. The R-40-25 class was very similar to the R-40-23 class except that the hardware - hinges, ladders, etc. - on the sides were painted orange instead of black. *(Lloyd Keyser collection)*

Below • Huntsville, Alabama in December 1969 is the date and place of this shot. PFE 4490, class R-40-25, series 2001 through 5000, has been repainted in the later gothic scheme used after 1961 however the reporting marks are not white and placed in a black field.
(Bernie Wooller)

Left • Some of the details worthy of note on this shot of PFE 4490 at Huntsville, Alabama in December 1969 is the high placement of the placard board (upper left), the rivet pattern along the seam and the light interior color which aids vision inside the otherwise very dark car. *(Bernie Wooller)*

Above • Three of the four hatches on PFE 4914, class R-40-25, series 2001 through 5000 built between 1949 and 1950 by Southern Pacific Equipment Company, are open for ventilation is this July 1974 of a dirty car. PFE cars were washed regularly until after World War Two when such began to occur less frequently. After 1955, according to Thompson in the second edition of *Pacific Fruit Express*, car washing essentially ended except for cars undergoing repairs or repainting. Notice the Miner D-3290 hand brake. *(George Berisso)*

Below • Class R-40-26, series 8001 through 10000, was the first class of PFE reefers to be delivered with a "plug" door and a six-foot door opening. This change was, at least in part, to accommodate the increased use of fork lifts for loading and unloading refrigerator cars. Class R-40-26 reefers were built in 1951 by Southern Pacific Equipment Company. PFE 8088 is seen in Huntsville, Alabama in October 1970. A note in the November 1973 *Official Railway Equipment Register* indicates these cars were equipped with Preco air circulating fans model AA-2 and were equipped for half stage icing service. *(Bernie Wooller)*

Right • PFE 9804, class R-40-26, series 8001 through 10000 built in 1951 by Southern Pacific Equipment Company, carries the basic paint and lettering scheme applied after 1961. The idea of the black patch in which the reporting marks are painted in white was to make this information easier to read on a very dirty car. Ends and roofs were supplied by Standard Railway Equipment Company. This shot was taken in June 1969 in Huntsville, Alabama.

(Bernie Wooller)

Above • Some R-40-26 refrigerator cars had the inside height increased from 7'-4" to 7'-10" about 1965 or 1966. When this occurred the cars were renumbered from series 8001 through 10000 into series 18001 through 19999. PFE 18366 was photographed during December 1970 at Huntsville, Alabama. *(Bernie Wooller)*

Below • PFE 61073 is being unloaded in Huntsville, Alabama in December 1972. A number of cars from class R-40-26, series 8001 through 10000 received "foam-in-place" floors about 1970 and were then renumbered into series 61000 through 61999. *(Bernie Wooller)*

Right • The usual reason for such a patchwork of clean areas on an otherwise dirty car was the result of the required periodic reweighing of cars, in this case at Nampa, Idaho in April 1970. PFE 66103 is another car which received new "foam-in-place" floors. This photo was taken in Huntsville, Alabama in September 1970.
(Bernie Wooller)

Above • When first built, PFE's 2000 class R-40-26 reefers were numbered 8001 through 10000 and was the first series of PFE reefers to be equipped with plug doors which were supplied by Youngstown. PFE had experimented with plug doors earlier. The entire series was built by Southern Pacific Equipment Company at the SP Los Angeles and Colton shops in California between July 1951 and May 1952. PFE 19931, seen in Fort Worth, Texas in November 1966 was built in April 1951 and rebuilt about 1965 to have the interior height increased and new floors and insulation installed. The paint on this car is fairly fresh and reflects some PFE practices that came some time after the car was built including the location of the name and heralds (1961), the black panel and white lettering for the reporting marks (1965) and the aluminum roof (1962). *(K.B. King, Jr., Lloyd Keyser collection)*

Below • Notice on PFE 10054, class R-40-27, series 10001 through 11700 built during June 1957 by Southern Pacific Equipment Company that it has a plug door AND hinges. The combination of a four foot wide plug door which slides to the left and a two foot wide hinged door on the right provides a six foot wide opening for loading and unloading but allows only a two foot wide opening so that less cold air is lost during inspection. The date and place of this photo are January 1975 and Huntsville, Alabama.
(Bernie Wooller)

Right • In Fort Worth, Texas in December 1979 we find PFE 10103, class R-40-27, series 10001 through 11700, built by Southern Pacific Equipment Company. This paint and lettering arrangement came into use in 1961.
(Lloyd Keyser collection)

Left • A surprisingly clean PFE 10591 is in Sacramento, California in November 1991.
(Lloyd Keyser collection)

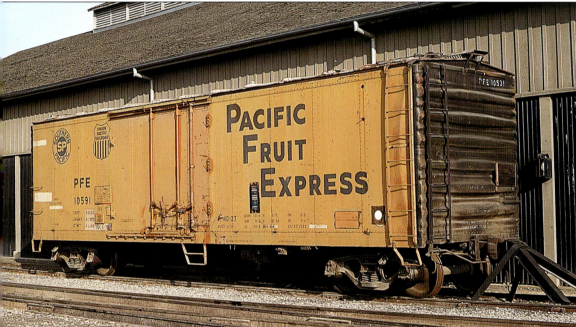

Below • This shot of PFE 10981, class R-40-27, taken in Huntsville, Alabama clearly shows how the combination of plug and hinged doors provided a six foot wide opening for loading or unloading or a two foot opening for inspection. The date is March 1971 and this car is part of series 10001 through 11700 built by Southern Pacific Equipment Company in 1957.
(Bernie Wooller)

Above • This offers a view of the roof of a class R-40-27 in Long Island City, New York on September 29, 1976. PFE 11269 has three hatches open, presumably for ventilation, but one hatch remains closed. Notice that while the car is very dirty the tops of the rungs on the ladder on the right are worn clean from frequent use. *(Matthew J. Herson, Jr. collection)*

Below • Class R-40-28, series 11701 through 11800, took the combination plug and hinged door one step farther by having a six foot wide plug door in addition to the two foot hinged door making a total door opening of eight feet. A good thing made better. PFE 11721 was built in 1957 by Southern Pacific Equipment Company and photographed in October 1978 at Fort Worth, Texas. *(Lloyd Keyser collection)*

Right • The 5000 reefers in class R-40-23 were delivered between January and October 1947. The order was apportioned among five builders - American Car & Foundry, General American, Mount Vernon, Pacific Car & Foundry and Pullman-Standard - with each builder producing 1000 cars for Pacific Fruit Express. These cars were numbered from 5001 through 8000 and 46703 through 48702 when first delivered. There is a diesel engine immediately adjacent to the near truck which might make one suspect that this is a mechanical reefer. It is not. These cars were distinctive in a number of respects including an all-welded underframe, extra height, an additional inch of insulation, Preco model FG-36 air circulating fans and sidewall flues to facilitate air circulation. In 1960 and 1961 one thousand of the cars from class R-40-23, including PFE 20305, built in February 1947 and seen here at the Orange Empire Railway Museum in Perris, California in July 1987, received diesel engines to power the air circulating fans when the car was standing still. The AAR mechanical designation remains RS or ice bunker refrigerator car. *(Lloyd Keyser collection)*

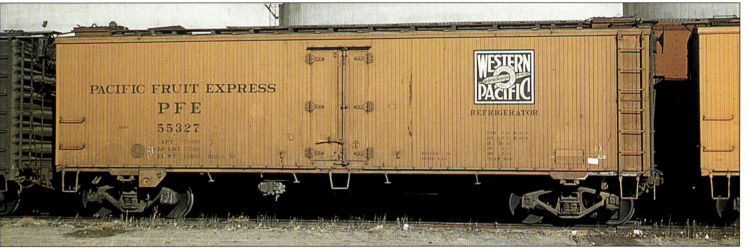

Above • PFE 55327, class R-30-9, series 55001 through 55900, was photographed in Council Bluffs, Iowa on November 5, 1955. These cars were owned by the Western Pacific but operated as part of the Pacific Fruit Express fleet and went everywhere. When the Western Pacific needed refrigerator cars the cars were supplied without regard to ownership so these cars could have been loaded anywhere Pacific Fruit Express operated. The relationship between the Western Pacific and Pacific Fruit Express ended in 1967. *(Lou Schmitz)*

Below • The book *Pacific Fruit Express*, Second Edition by Thompson, Church and Jones explains in detail the history of the PFE cars bearing the Western Pacific herald. PFE reserved the number series 55001 to 55900 for Western Pacific owned refrigerator cars which were reconditioned in 1953 and 1954. Originally built by AC&F in 1923 for the Western Pacific in anticipation of a contract between WP and PFE, there were 2775 cars built to PFE design R-30-13 and first numbered for PFE in series 50001 to 52775. When reconditioned the first time after 1938 the reconditioned cars were changed to class R-30-9 as on this car. Indeed, according to the reference cited above, 114 cars lasted until 1950 without being reconditioned. Because of the Western Pacific's unwillingness to have these cars rebuilt, instead of merely reconditioned, they managed to retain an appearance much like when new in 1923. Most of these cars were probably gone by about 1960. Fort Worth, Texas *(Lloyd Keyser collection)*

RAILWAY EXPRESS AGENCY

In an earlier era one shipped small packages with the Railway Express Agency (REA) in the same way that one now patronizes United Parcel Service. Cars of REA could be seen in most important passenger trains. Every station agent of virtually every railroad in the country was also an agent of the Railway Express Agency. The ubiquitous green trucks with red wheels of the REA were seen in practically every corner of the United States.

The Railway Express Agency was formed 1929 by a number of the most important railroads in the country as a successor to American Railway Express Agency which was itself a merger of a number of smaller, regional express companies operated by railroads and other businesses. As the railroads began removing passenger trains from their schedules in the late 1950s and early 1960s so too did the business conducted by REA begin to contract. By the mid-1970s REA was, for all practical purposes gone.

Right • This is the classic Railway Express Agency express refrigerator car remembered by the old-timers. The wood siding, arched roof and large diamond shaped logo are instantly recognizable. Most of the time REA reefers were operated in passenger trains and were equipped with high speed trucks, passenger air and steam lines and other features necessary for the car's inclusion in a passenger train consist. REX 1253 (BR), series 1237 through 1278, was leased from General American Transportation Corporation. The lease for this car began in 1943 but whether the car was new then or had been in service for sometime is not known. These cars may have come to REA from General American's GARX series 900 through 999 which had the same dimensions as the REX series 1237 through 1278. This car remained in service as late as 1963. This shot was taken in September 1961 east of Union Station in Columbus, Ohio. *(Paul C. Winters)*

Below • REX 7141 (BR), series 6900 through 7399, was built in 1955 by General American Transportation Corporation. This photo was taken in the Pennsylvania Railroad's Spruce Street coach yard in Columbus, Ohio in March 1962. *(Paul C. Winters)*

Above • REX 7769 (BR), series 7400 through 7899, was one of 500 similar cars built for the Railway Express Agency in 1957 by General American Transportation Corporation. This group of cars was among the last ice bunker refrigerator cars built in the United States. This car was photographed in Middletown, Pennsylvania in September 1989. *(George F. Melvin)*

Below • The heritage of REX 6713 (BR), series 6600 through 6799, is obviously that of a World War Two troop sleeper built by Pullman-Standard. The first car of this series was on the REA roster by April of 1950. Our photograph dates from July 17, 1980 in Chicago, Illinois.
(James Mischke)

SWIFT

Swift operated their own fleet of refrigerator, stock and tank cars, among which were twenty reefers lettered for Plankinton Packing Company which was located in Milwaukee, Wisconsin, as well as a few gondolas and flat cars for intra-plant use until 1930 when the refrigerator and tank cars were sold to GATC and leased back to Swift.

In the years leading up to 1948 most Swift reefers were yellow with black lettering. In 1947 some Swift reefers had a large red "Swift" on the right half of the yellow side. In 1948 a white "Swift" appeared in a large red field on the right half of the side. Next, about 1950, came the bright red reefers with white lettering. The silver cars with "Swift" inside a red rectangle or "Swift Premium" inside a red circle can be documented as early as 1959.

Significant numbers of Swift wood reefers were rebuilt during the 1940s and early 1950s. Apparently all were renumbered at the time of rebuilding. This resulted in new number series appearing in the *Official Railway Equipment Register*s while photos reveal cars with characteristics similar to those built during the 1920s. By April 1978 there remained only one car in the 25000 series bearing the SRLX reporting marks.

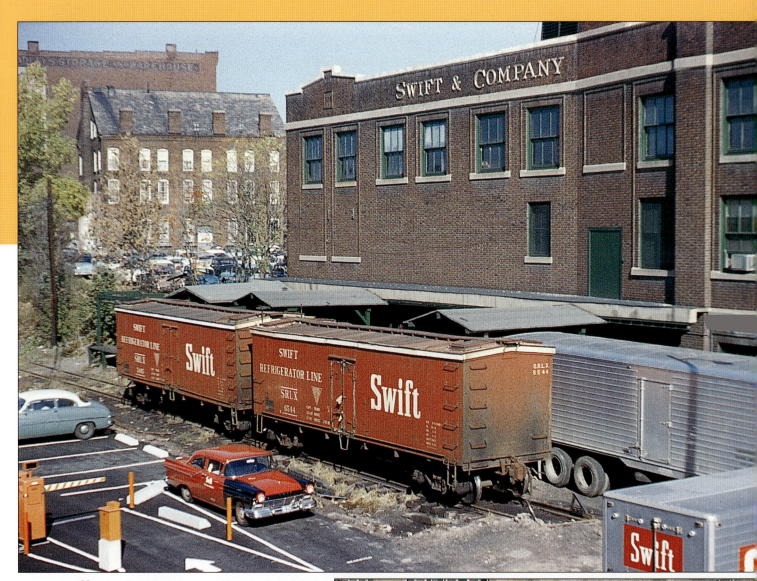

Above • Swift had a variety of large and small facilities in various parts of the country. The New York, New Haven and Hartford served this plant in Hartford, Connecticutt seen here in 1957. The nearest Swift reefer, SRLX 6544 was rebuilt in the early 1950s and was repainted bright red at that time.
(J. W. Swanberg)

Right • In 1948 only four cars remained in Swift reefer series 1700 through 1799 so, by 1955 when this photo was taken in Tampa, Florida, SRLX 1755, seen here, may well have been the last car of the series. *(K.B. King, Jr, Lloyd Keyser collection)*

Above • Reefers in series 2500 through 2874 began to appear in the early 1940s, no doubt as rebuilds from some other similar series. SRLX 2778 is in Lawrence, Kansas in July 1955. These were designated as RSM (ice bunkers and meat rails) and had inside partitions. *(Don Ball)*

Below • Series 3300 through 5199 began appearing in the very early 1940s. The total number of cars in the series continued to increase until 1950. This increase suggests a rebuilding program which ended about 1950. SRLX 5042 is equipped with brine tanks and meat rails (RAM) and is seen here in December 1955 in Lawrence, Kansas. *(Don Ball)*

Left • The old and the new are together in this string of reefers passing the photographer in January 1961. Wood-sheathed SRLX 2634 was part of the series 2500 through 2874 and carries the red paint applied from about 1950 onward while steel-sheathed SRLX 15097 bears the silver paint first used in 1959.

(Emery J. Gulash, Morning Sun Books collection)

Above • The old is new in the case of SRLX 5156, originally built in the 1920s, which was painted in Swift's latest paint scheme at the GATC East Chicago shops in 1961. This shot was taken in August 1972 after the car became part of the collection of the National Railroad Museum in Green Bay, Wisconsin. *(Rail Data Services collection)*

Below • As part of a rebuilding and renumbering program begun just before or during World War II, SRLX 5237, built in January 1928, was rebuilt in 1951. Work was probably completed in May of that year. This car was part of number series 5200 through 5799. By 1966 almost all these cars had been retired. Only two cars remained in an expanded number series of 3500 through 6099.

(Jim Konas, Randy Garnhart collection)

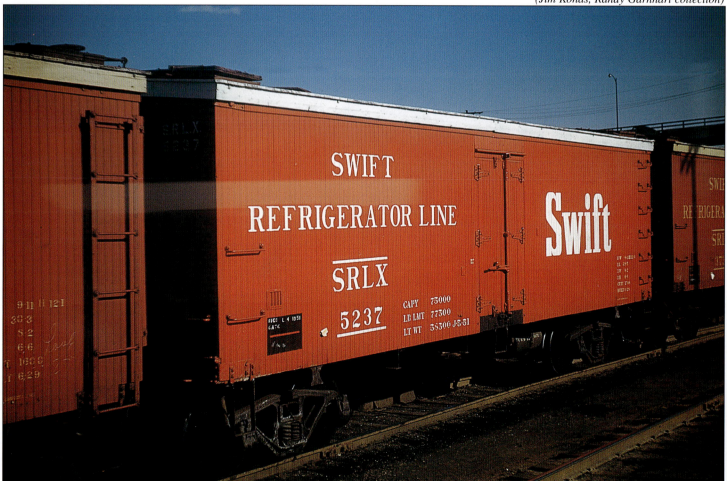

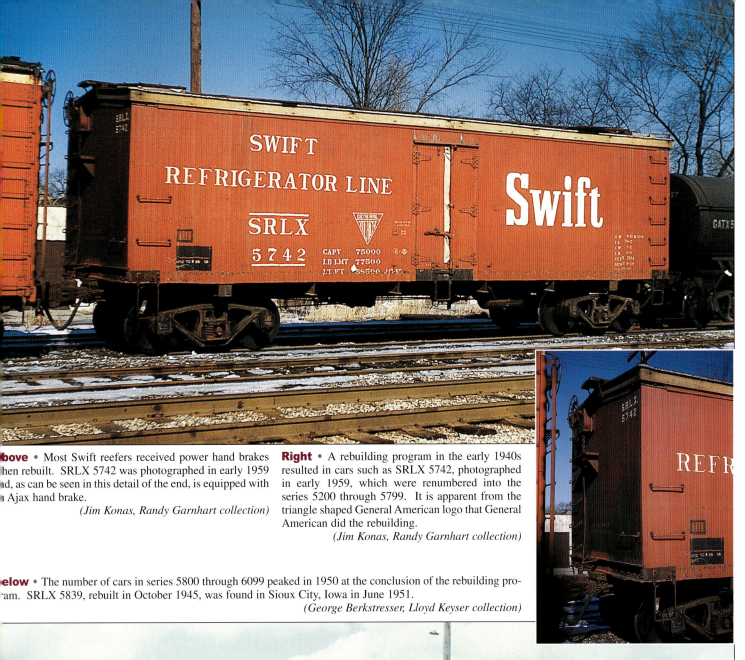

Above • Most Swift reefers received power hand brakes when rebuilt. SRLX 5742 was photographed in early 1959 and, as can be seen in this detail of the end, is equipped with an Ajax hand brake.
(Jim Konas, Randy Garnhart collection)

Right • A rebuilding program in the early 1940s resulted in cars such as SRLX 5742, photographed in early 1959, which were renumbered into the series 5200 through 5799. It is apparent from the triangle shaped General American logo that General American did the rebuilding.
(Jim Konas, Randy Garnhart collection)

Below • The number of cars in series 5800 through 6099 peaked in 1950 at the conclusion of the rebuilding program. SRLX 5839, rebuilt in October 1945, was found in Sioux City, Iowa in June 1951.
(George Berkstresser, Lloyd Keyser collection)

Above • SRLX 15392, from series 15000 through 17399, was built in June 1954 by General American and was photographed in Sioux City, Iowa later that same year. *(George Berkstresser, Lloyd Keyser collection)*

Below • All-steel reefers began to supplant the wood fleet in the 1950s. SRLX 15597, shown here at Omaha, Nebraska August 20, 1956 was built in June 1954 by General American. *(Lou Schmitz)*

Above • SRLX 15692 is in Bensonville, Illinois in April 1961. By this time all-steel cars were being painted in the silver paint but this car, built in June 1954 by General American retains its original paint scheme. *(Rail Data Services collection)*

Above • Cars in series 15000 through 17399 were equipped with brine tanks. The brine tank drains are easily seen over each truck in this view of SRLX 15350 which was built in June 1954. *(Paul C. Winters)*

Below • Compare the Swift logo in the rectangular field with the Swift's Premium logo in the red circle. SRLX 15116 was built in 1954 by GATC for the Swift fleet. This silver paint job was applied in 1959 or earlier and photographed in May 1960.

(Jim Konas, Randy Garnhart collection)

Above • SRLX 15248 and SRLX 15116 in the preceding photo were part of series 15000 through 17399 which were built in 1954 by General American. All cars in this series were equipped with brine tanks and had meat rails. Photo taken May 1960. Originally delivered in red, these cars have been repainted in the current silver paint scheme. *(Jim Konas, Randy Garnhart collection)*

Below • The Miner 3290-XL power hand brake is easily identifie on SRLX 15801 which was built in November 1956 by GATC a part of series 15000 through 17399. The car seen here was ph tographed in Milwaukee, Wisconsin in February 1968.
(Rail Data Services collectio

Left • From SRLX 2571 on the left we see a string of cars outside Swifts large plant in Sioux City, Iowa in 1951. All six reefers visible here are wood-sheathed. Steel-sheathed reefers for Swift are still in the future. The billboard on top of the building in the distance at right says "Swift's Brookfield Sausage" while the side of the building bears the legend "Swift & Company."
(George Berkstresser, Lloyd Keyser collection)

Above • Refrigerator cars for the transportation of meat and related products had to be clean and in good repair before loading. The photo above, taken in Sioux City, Iowa in September 1954, shows Swift's small yard for storage and car servicing. The tracks in the background appear to be for storage of cars while the two tracks in the foreground separated by the loading dock appear to be for servicing and cleaning of cars. Most of the cars in both photos on this page appear to be those with steel underframes and wood superstructures but a new all-steel car stands out prominently in the foreground. One yellow car seems to have escaped being repainted into the bright red, the use of which began about 1950. What appears to be pallets on the dock are more likely floor racks. Floor racks provided the necessary space below a refrigerated load for the proper circulation of air so that the desired temperature could more easily be maintained throughout the car's contents.

(George Berkstresser photo, Lloyd Keyser collection)

Below • Sioux City was one of the large Midwestern meat packing centers and, at the time of this photo, Swift, Cudahy and Armour all had large meat packing plants in the vicinity of the Sioux City Stock Yards Company. The Milwaukee Road, Great Northern, Sioux City Terminal Railway which was owned by the Sioux City Stock Yards Company and Chicago & North Western subsidiary Chicago, St. Paul, Minneapolis & Omaha all had extensive yards in the vicinity of the stock yards for handling inbound livestock and outbound meat and other products of the meat packing industry. This second view of the same facility as above, also from September 1954, shows the few buildings necessary to carry out the car servicing done here. Tank cars also carried meat packing byproducts such as lard, lard oil, tallow, and fats. *(George Berkstresser photo, Lloyd Keyser collection)*

UNION REFRIGERATOR TRANSIT
A Division of General American Transportation Corporation
Milwaukee, Wisconsin

Union Refrigerator Transit (URTL) was founded in Milwaukee, Wisconsin in 1903, unrelated to an earlier Kentucky company of the same name. URTX had in 1903 a fleet of 1726 cars. In 1929 URTL was acquired by General American and had at that time almost 5000 cars. URTL continued to operate separately from General American until some time around 1970 when all URTL cars were integrated into the General American listings. All freight cars with URTX reporting marks were out of service before 1988.

It appears that URTX reefers were renumbered each time they were leased to a new lessee or assigned to a particular service making it difficult to trace the cars through the *Official Railway Equipment Registers* from year to year. In addition to private companies, URTX leased large numbers of reefers to the Milwaukee Road and the SOO Line as well as smaller numbers of cars to the Chicago Great Western, the Minneapolis & St. Louis and perhaps other railroads as well.

Right • In 1955 General American rebuilt quite a number of cars originally built in October 1931. Wood ends were replaced with square-cornered Dreadnaught ends and geared hand brakes replaced the old vertical staff hand brakes. URTX 1806 (RS), series 1000 through 2999, was in New Lisbon, Wisconsin on August 9, 1969 for this picture. *(Rail Data Services collection)*

Below • Quite a number of the old reefers from 1931 were rebuilt in 1955 and leased to the SOO Line. Most were numbered in the 1800s. URTX 1840 (RS), series 1000 through 2999, is one of those leased to the SOO and see here on April 17, 197 in New Lisbon, Wisconsin. *(Rail Data Services collection)*

Above • URTX 1878 (RS), series 1000 through 2999, built by General American in October 1931 and rebuilt in 1955 is seen here in March 1968. *(Paul C. Winters)*

Below • URTX 1944 (RS), built October 1931 by General American and rebuilt in November 1955, traveled all the way to Huntsville, Alabama for this photo taken some time after July 1967. *(Bernie Wooller)*

Left • Binghamton, New York is the location of this July 1972 photo of URTX 1973 (RS), series 1000 through 2999. Details of the end and Universal hand brake are easily seen in this shot. *(Dick Argo)*

Above • MERX 422 and URTX 1995 (RS), series 1000 through 2999, and in Columbus, Ohio on February 10, 1963. This reefer is another of the 500 refrigerator cars built in 1930 and 1931 and rebuilt in 1955. The original number series was 88000 through 88499. *(Paul C. Winters)*

Below • We're back in Binghamton, New York in March 1970 where we find URTX 2016 (RS), series 1000 through 2999. As can be seen, the cars built in 1931 and rebuilt in 1955 remained in service long after most refrigerator lines were using mostly all steel equipment. *(Rail Data Services collection)*

Right • The Minneapolis & St. Louis adopted the angled *The Peoria Gateway* slogan for the side of freight cars in November 1937 and the slogan appeared on URTX reefers shortly thereafter. URTX 4697 was photographed in Lawrence, Kansas in September 1955.
(Don Ball)

Right • The round three-color M&StL herald was in use in 1930 or perhaps earlier and was used on refrigerator and stock cars leased from General American. URTX 4975, built in August 1930, is pretty much in original condition in this view on August 16, 1962 in Rochester, Minnesota. The small angle irons across the bottom of the sides were often added to cars with vertical exterior wood sheathing to hold the bottoms of the boards in place as the nails began to loosen. *(Bruce Black)*

Above • The Minneapolis & St. Louis leased a few refrigerator cars from URTX in the 1950s. URTX 4802 (RS), series 4800 through 4899, was built in October 1931 and rebuilt in 1955 as evidenced by the steel, square-cornered Dreadnaught ends and power hand brake. The stencil arrangement on the right half was adopted by the M&StL in 1956 and is still in very good condition in this November 1967 view. *(Rail Data Services collection)*

Below • It is not clear whether all the cars in the series 4800 through 4899 were leased to the M&StL or not. URTX 4816 (RS), series 4800 through 4899, was built in October 1931 by General American rebuilt in May 1955. Some of the changes included the steel, square-corner Dreadnaught ends and Universal power hand brake seen in this shot taken in Binghampton, New York during July 1972. Notice the lower position of the white stripe as compared to the stripe on the side of URTX 4802 seen in the previous photograph. *(Dick Argo)*

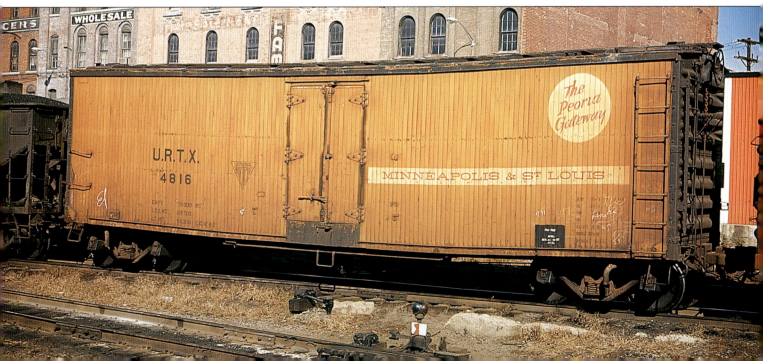

Above • Compare URTX 5093 (RS), series 5000 through 5099, seen here in 1956 in San Bernardino, California with the reefer in the previous photo to compare the original appearance and the rebuilt appearance of these General American built refrigerator cars. *(K. B. King, Jr., Lloyd Keyser collection)*

Below • Although built in March 1941 on a steel underframe, URTX 5169 (RSM), series 5100 through 5174, has the appearance of a much older refrigerator car. When new this reefer was equipped with the Equipco 3140 hand brake seen here. The switcher on the left belongs to the Chicago Great Western. *(Jim Konas, Randy Garnhart collection)*

Above • URTX 5366 (RSM), series 5200 through 5499, was built in 1941 and is typical of 200 cars with Duryea cushioned underframes built by General American for Union Refrigerator Transit (165 cars) and GARX (35 cars). By 1941 other builders were using steel ends on reefers if not both steel ends and sides. This car, photographed at San Bernardino, California in November 1958, is reminiscent of refrigerator car construction from the 1920s and early 1930s. *(K. B. King, Jr., Lloyd Keyser collection)*

Below • It is April 1951 in Omaha, Nebraska and we have a chance to see URTX 5861 (RS) before rebuilding. Notice the wooden ends and vertical staff hand brake.

(Lloyd Keyser collection)

Left • URTX 37055 (RS), series 37000 through 37449, built October 1940 by General American is one of the earlier versions of refrigerator cars built with the horizontal seam along the center of the sides. This design feature was incorporated into refrigerator cars built by several different freight car manufacturing companies including General American, Pressed Steel Car. Co., and American Car and Foundry. This example, photographed in October 1964, was built in October 1948.

(Rail Data Services collection)

Top • General American built series 37000 through 37974 in 1951. This example, URTX 37358 (RS), was built in June 1951. This photo dates from October 1967.
(Randy Garnhart, Randy Garnhart collection)

Center • A freshly painted URTX 37397 (RS), series 37000 through 37974, was in Lawrence, Kansas in June 1956.
(Don Ball collection)

Bottom • The lighting of this August 31, 1980 photo makes it easy to see the drain pipes over each truck. URTX 37453 (RS), series 37000 through 37974, was built in June 1949 by General American.
(Matthew J. Herson, Jr. collection)

Above • URTX 38109 (RS), series 38100 through 40899, was found in Othello, Washington on February 16, 1973. This car was built in December 1954 by General American and is equipped for half stage icing and has air circulating fans. *(Wade Stevenson)*

Below • Sometimes a good photo is the result of being in the right place at the right time as was the case of this shot of URTX 60422 (RSM), series 60200 through 60524, built by General American and photographed in July 1966. *(Emery J. Gulash, Morning Sun Books collection)*

Above and Inset • Sioux City Dressed Beef, located in Sioux City, Iowa, was a division of Needham Packing Company. URTX 60441 (RSM), series 60200 through 60524, was built in September 1954 by General American. This shot was taken on October 19, 1963 in Council Bluffs, Iowa. When Cudahy's plant in Sioux City closed in 1954 Sioux City Dressed Beef began operation. *(both, Lou Schmitz)*

Below • Sioux City, Iowa was one of the great meat packing centers in the U.S. and had large plants belonging to Armour, Cudahy and Swift. URTX 60680 (RSM), series 60680 through 60699, was photographed on February 10, 1963 in Columbus, Ohio.
(Paul C. Winters)

Below • Compare this photo of URTX 60726 (RSM), series 60701 through 60749, with the previous shot of URTX 60680 which was also leased to Raskin. This photo was taken February 2, 1963 in Council Bluffs, Iowa while the preceding one was taken eight days later and a few hundred miles away. Which color is correct - yellow or orange? What accounts for the difference between the views - film, weather, processing, or something else? *(Lou Schmitz)*

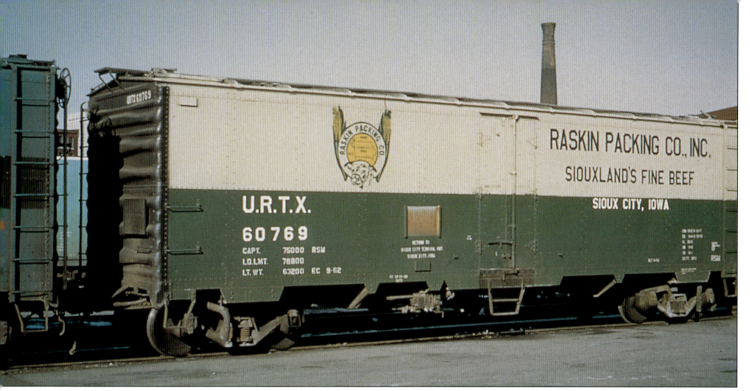

Above • URTX 60769 (RSM), series 60750 through 62999, was photographed in Sioux City, Iowa in 1969. This car were built in 1954 by General American and repainted in this cream and green scheme in 1962. *(The Houser collection)*

Below • Dubuque Packing leased URTX 63016 (RSM), series 63000 through 63049. Often the date built is legible in a photo but not in this case. Power hand brakes were required on cars built after January 1, 1937 so this car with its vertical staff hand brake was built before then. The car was repainted in 1958 and photographed in May 1960. *(Jim Konas, Randy Garnhart collection)*

Left • This shot taken in Tampa, Florida in 1956 illustrates how wide ranging refrigerator cars could be. A car with wooden ends and a power hand brake suggests either a rebuilt car or one built after 1936. Replacement of a vertical staff hand brake with a power hand brake is unlikely. URTX 63216 (RSM), series 63200 through 63249, had adjustable ice grates for stage icing. *(K. B. King, Jr., Lloyd Keyser collection)*

Above • URTX 63347 (RSM), series 63000 through 63454, is in Bensonville, Illinois in March 1961. Notice the lighter color boards at the left end of the side. Is this evidence of a recent repair? *(Rail Data Services collection)*

Below • URTX 63461 (RSM), series 63455 through 63499, was built in Jun 1950 by General American. This August 1969 shot in Dubuque, Iowa shows ve clean paint. The car was very likely repainted the last time a new light weight wa stenciled on the car in may 1966. *(Randy Garnhart)*

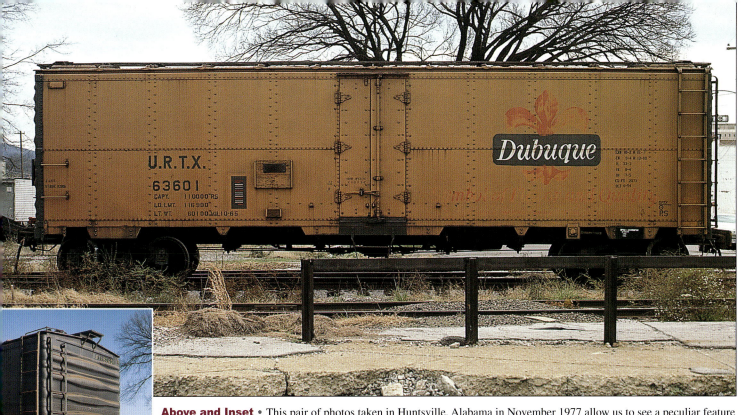

Above and Inset • This pair of photos taken in Huntsville, Alabama in November 1977 allow us to see a peculiar feature of many all steel refrigerator cars. Notice that the small ribs on the end do not occur between all of the large ribs on these Improved Dreadnaught ends. Modelers have termed this style end the "Partnaught" end. URTX 63601 (RS) was built in August 1954 by General American. Even though this car is assigned to a meat packer it is a regular refrigerator car with ice bunkers but no meat rails. Notice how red fades faster than other colors. *(Bernie Wooller)*

Below • General American built URTX 63648 (RS), series 63625 through 63749, in December 1954. This photo was taken in Council Bluffs, Iowa on July 22, 1962. This car was most likely repainted at the same time a new light weight was stenciled on the car in General American's East Chicago, Indiana shops in April 1962. *(Lou Schmitz)*

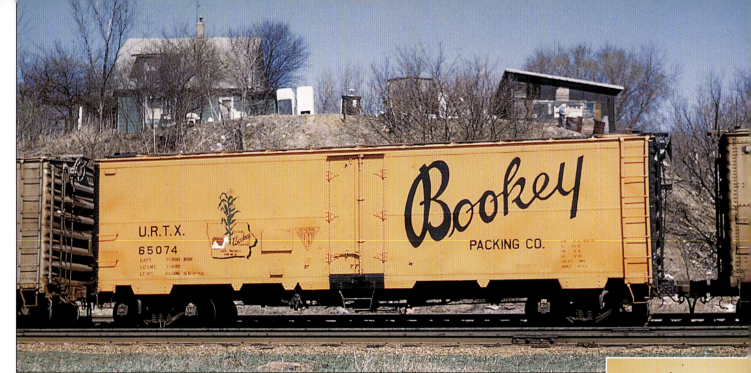

Above and Inset Right • URTX 65074 (RSM), series 65065 through 65074, was built September 1954 by General American and photographed April 6, 1963 in Des Moines, Iowa where Bookey Packing Company was located. *(Lou Schmitz)*

Below • General American bought the Rock Island's refrigerator car fleet in 1933. Those cars are long gone, of course, but the Rock Island still needed for a few refrigerator cars. URTX 67002 (RSM), series 67000 through 67099 was painted for the Rock Island in 1964 and photographed on July 9, 1967 in Council Bluffs, Iowa. The namesake bluffs are visible behind the car. *(Lou Schmitz)*

Below • URTX 67075 (RSM), series 67000 through 67099, was photographed September 1957 in Council Bluffs, Iowa. *(Lou Schmitz)*

Above • Plain old reefers with no special lettering seldom get photographed so we are lucky to have this shot of URTX 68038 (RSM), series 67925 through 68099. This reefer with meat rails was built in 1954 and painted in 1966.
(Morning Sun Books collection)

Below • This car was built by General American in 1954. URTX 68064 (RSM) was photographed in San Bernardino, California in 1957.
(K. B. King, Jr., Lloyd Keyser collection)

Above • Producers Packing Company, Garden City, Kansas, packers of Farmbest Beef, is just one of the many small meat packers the filled the vacuum left when Armour, Cudahy and Swift closed their large Midwestern plants. URTX 68172 (RSM), series 68100 through 69049, was built in June 1960 by General American. This photo dates from April 1968.
(Rail Data Services collection)

Below • MID (Minnesota, Iowa, Dakota) Packing Company of Luverne Minnesota was one of many small meat packing companies leasing a few mea reefers from Union Refrigerator Transit. URTX 69222 (RSM), series 6920 through 69232, was built July 1950 by General American and photographed i Council Bluffs, Iowa on October 14, 1962. *(Lou Schmitz)*

Right • Surely this qualifies as a 'billboard' paint scheme. Twenty URTX reefers like URTX 72214 (RSM), series 72201 through 72220, were painted for the Marhoefer Packing Company of Muncie, Indiana which was served by the Nickel Plate Road. These reefers, iced at the Marhoefer facility by The City Ice Company before loading, could be seen all over the United States and this one is seen here in Council Bluffs, Iowa on January 25, 1964. The cars, retired in 1969, were outfitted with Miner X-3290 hand brakes.
(Lou Schmitz)

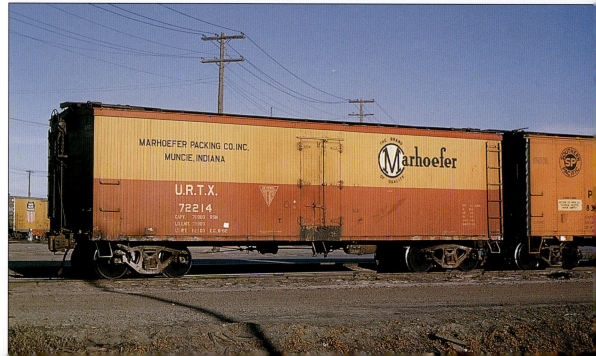

Below • URTX 72722 (RSM), series 72718 through 72729, was built in October 1948 by General American. Some of the equipment at the left end of the car suggests this car is at the RIP (repair in place) track on March 30, 1970, in Othello, Washington. *(Wade Stevenson)*

Below and Inset • Iowa Beef Packers, Inc. (IBP) is generally credited with changing the face of the meat packing business in the United States. Whether you view IBP as masters of efficiency or union 'busters' by the year 2000 IBP had 33% of the beef packing business. URTX 73332 (RSM), series 73325 through 74999, built in September 1954 by General American was photographed in Council Bluffs, Iowa on October 31, 1964. *(Lou Schmitz)*

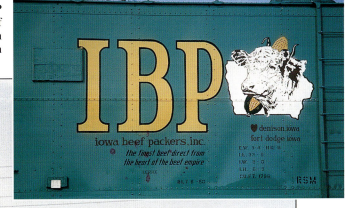

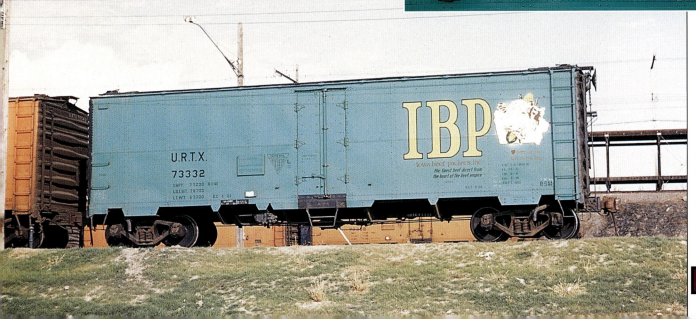

Right • URTX 73300 (RSM), series 73300 through 73324, was photographed in Endicott, New York in September 1969. URTX 60442 is the next car to the right. General American built cars with this straight side sill from about 1948 through 1950.
(Rail Data Services collection)

Below • URTX 73317 (RSM), series 73300 through 73324 was in Columbus, Ohio in October 1969. Both this car and the one above are marked "NOT FOR CHUNK ICE." *(Dick Argo)*

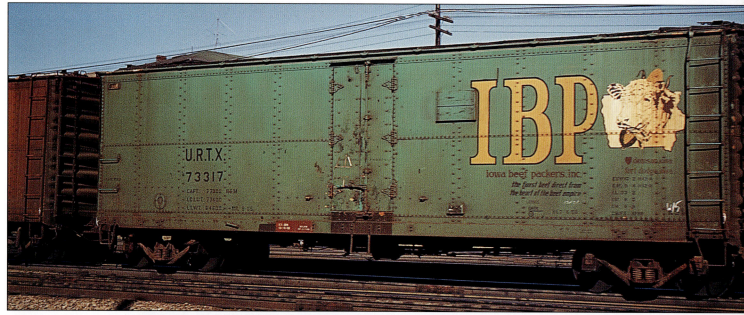

Right • URTX 73303 (RSM), series 73300 through 73324, built June 1950 by General American, appears blue to us but you may see it as green. This shot was taken on April 17, 1965 in Council Bluffs, Iowa.
(Lou Schmitz)

Left • It is June 1971 and URTX 75551 (RSM), series 75550 through 75999, leased to American Beef Packers Inc. rolls past the photographer in Endicott, New York.
(Rail Data Services collection)

WESTERN REFRIGERATOR LINE COMPANY

Green Bay, Wisconsin

Western Refrigerator Line (WRX) provided refrigerator cars for the Green Bay & Western Railroad Company but shared some officers with North Western Refrigerator Line. The Western Refrigerator Line operated a small number of cars. Typically there were 400 to 500 refrigerator cars in one to three number series in operation at any one time. In 1953 and 1954 WRX had but one number series and only 400 refrigerator cars. This one number series - 9000 through 9999 is the only one for which we have photos. The majority of WRX cars, but never more than 435, were always in this series so, as will be seen, we have nice coverage of this small refrigerator car operator.

Above • WRX 9032 (RS), from the original 1932 series 9000 through 9449, has a couple of unusual features worth noting. Notice how the side sills are quite deep between the two trucks. The Klasing power hand brake has a vertical shaft and small hand wheel above the top of the car. Normally power hand brake wheels protrude from the car end on a horizontal shaft. This odd hand brake was in production (1930) before this series of cars was built between 1932 and 1936. This shot dates from July 1963 in Dallas, Texas.
(Lloyd Keyser collection)

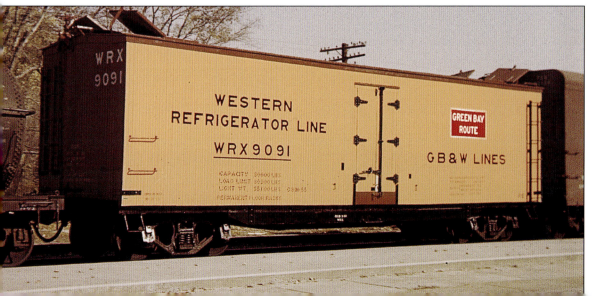

Left • The relationship between Western Refrigerator Line and the Green Bay & Western Railroad was intended to be obvious as indicated by the lettering on the right half of the car sides. WRX 9091 (RS), series 9000 through 9449, was photographed during November 1955 in Lawrence, Kansas.
(Don Ball)

Above • WRX 9519 (RS), series 9000 through 9999, was renumbered from the 10,000 series when permanent floor racks were installed sometime between 1932 and 1937. This March 1968 photo shows WRX 9519 in between two much larger, more modern refrigerator cars in Hammond, Indiana. *(Dr. Art Peterson)*

Below • WRX 9657 (RS), series 9000 through 9999, was photographed in Chicago, Illinois during October 1970. Notice that all these wood-sided WRX reefers have doors that are five feet wide instead of the more usual four feet.
(Owen Leander, Lloyd Keyser collection)

Right • WRX 9000 was built July 1936 and rebuilt in July 1954. The Murphy end and fishbelly underframe are good clues to the rebuilding. This car has eight hatches on the roof instead of the usual four. Notice that the sliding, plug door reaches almost all the way up to the roof suggesting that the overhead ice tanks are likely no longer in use. This car is labeled for dry blood loading and is stenciled "WHEN EMPTY RETURN TO AGENT C&NW RY" and, on the right side, "ARMOUR & COMPANY, Green Bay, Wisc." Our photographer made this exposure on July 13, 1975 in Sioux City, Iowa.
(Lou Schmitz)

WILSON CAR LINES
Division of Wilson & Company, Inc.
Green Bay, Wisconsin

Wilson and Company had packing plants in all the largest meat packing centers as well as smaller towns in various parts of the nation including Albert Lea, Minnesota, Cedar Rapids, Iowa, Chicago, Illinois, Columbus, Georgia, Denver, Colorado, Dothan, Alabama, Kansas City, Kansas, Oklahoma City, Oklahoma, Omaha, Nebraska and South Omaha, Nebraska. Wilson reefers could be seen all over the United States delivering their products for consumption in every corner of the country. Wilson operated their own fleet of refrigerator cars as well as a few stock cars and tank cars until the mid-1940s after which Wilson operated only refrigerator cars. Wilson also leased refrigerator cars from Mather in 1931 and 1932. Wilson and Company also leased refrigerator cars to other small meat packers. The Wilson and Company refrigerator car fleet reached its zenith in the mid-1950s with approximately 1500 cars. In the years following the number of cars in the Wilson and Company fleet declined rapidly. By 1981 there was no listing in the *Official Railway Equipment Register* for Wilson and Company or for cars with WCLX reporting marks.

Above • WCLX 9350 (RSM), series 8101 through 9600, has been stenciled as being built in 1950 and, indeed, the number series 8101-9299 was expanded in 1950 to include WCLX 9350 and other cars numbered above 9299. A new car of this design is unlikely. A rebuilt car is much more likely given the overall length of 36 feet. This photo was taken in Cedar Rapids, Iowa during October 1961. *(Lloyd Keyser)*

Right • This view of the end of WCLX 9350 (RSM) affords an examination of a few details. Notice the lack of a visible end sill. The brine drain can be seen hanging down immediately in front of the journal box. *(Lloyd Keyser)*

Right • WCLX 9458 (RSM), series 8101 through 9600, was partially photographed in the early 1950s at an unknown location. This car is equipped with AB brakes. The cars is this series had an overall length of 36 feet.
(K. B. King, Jr., Lloyd Keyser collection)

Below • WCLX 9556 (RSM), series 8101 through 9600, was photographed in May 1960. This car has a steel underframe, power hand brake and AB air brakes. Compare the size of the logo in this photo with the previous photo.
(Jim Konas, Randy Garnhart collection)

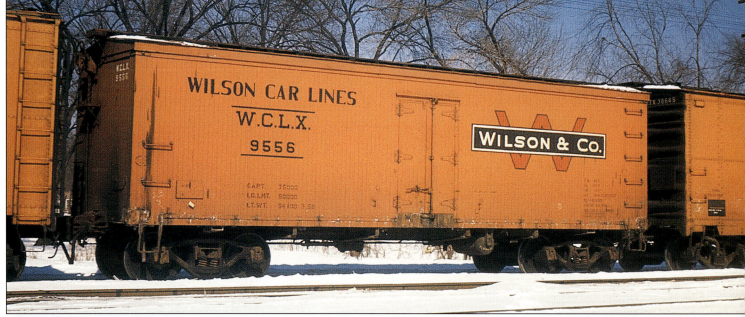

Above • Wilson and Company could not rely on short, wood cars forever but they did hold out a long time before beginning to acquire 40 foot steel cars. WCLX 2042 (RSM), series 2000 through 2799, was built in May 1957 and was photographed January 15, 1967 in Council Bluffs, Iowa
(Lou Schmitz)

Above • WCLX 2478 (RSM), series 2000 through 2799, was built in November 1957 and was photographed in Huntsville, Alabama in November 1970. *(Bernie Wooller)*

Below • WCLX 2585 (RSM), series 2000 through 2799, was photographed in Dallas, Texas in November 1968. *(Lloyd Keyser)*

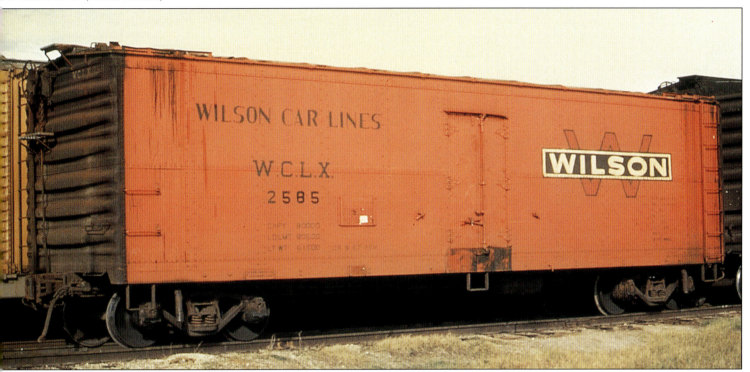

Below • With an overall length of 56 feet, 6 inches and a volume between bulkheads of 2475 cubic feet, the 5000 through 5184 series was the largest ice-bunker refrigerator car in the Wilson and Company fleet. There were originally 185 cars in this series. WCLX 5106 (RSM) was photographed in May 1972 at an unknown location. *(Paul C. Winters)*

Above • Some WCLX cars were semi-permanently coupled in pairs and renumbered. WCLX 1013A and 1013B (RSM) is an example of these paired refrigerator cars. With the namesake bluffs in the background these cars were photographed along the Missouri River in Council Bluffs, Iowa on May 31, 1971. *(Lou Schmitz)*

Below • WCLX 2024 (RSM), series 2000 through 2799, was buil[t] May 1957. Beefland International was located in Council Bluffs Iowa where this shot was taken on March 15, 1970. *(Lou Schmitz)*

Right • Cars leased to Schuyler Packing Company included WCLX 2099 (RSM) part of series 2000 through 2799. WCLX 2099 was photographed at an unknown location in January 1969.

(The Houser collection)

126

Above • Also leased to Schuyler Parking Company, WCLX 2115 was in Council Bluffs, Iowa on April 20, 1969 when the photo below was taken. *(Lou Schmitz)*

Below • Built in June 1957, WCLX 2202 (RSM), series 2000 through 2799, is leased to Needham Packing Company, Inc whose product brand was Flavorland Meats. This car was in Council Bluffs, Iowa on November 24, 1968. *(Lou Schmitz)*

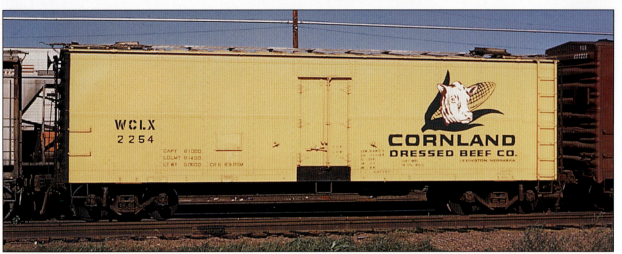

Left • On August 9 1969 in Council Bluffs, Iowa WCLX 2254 series 2000 through 2799 posed for this photograph. The car, built in June 1957, is leased to Cornland Dressed Beef Company in Lexington, Nebraska.

(Lou Schmitz)

EPILOGUE

A Wabash switcher and transfer caboose trundle by with three ART reefers at the 21st Street Interlocking in Chicago, Illinois in May 1954. The two reefers behind the caboose have steel sides and ends while the rear reefer has wood sides and ends. This slide represents the end of an era. No, it represents the end of many things related to railroads. The Wabash is long gone. The long Pennsylvania Railroad streamliner crossing the bridge in the background is no longer. The use of cabooses has almost completely ended. To be sure, we hear reports of a caboose in use here or there but to go out trackside and expect a wave from a friendly crew member in a caboose, that's gone! Ice bunker refrigerator cars are a thing of the past. It is all mechanical refrigeration now. Once in a while when one is trackside one hears the sound of a diesel engine running on one of the mechanical reefers but that is no replacement for the hustle of icing a string of ice bunker reefers. Besides, except for the paint, they all seem to look alike nowadays. We hope you enjoyed this look back at a bygone era and that the memories brought back were all happy ones of days when railroading was still being done in the time honored way by men who took pride in their work.

(Emery J. Gulash, Morning Sun Books collection)